D1486899

LIFE ISSUES

JUVENILE VIOLENCE

by Renardo Barden

Marshall Cavendish
NEW YORK • LONDON • TORONTO • SYDNEY

PUBLIC LIBRARY, PLAINFIELD, N.J.

364.36
B23

Published by Marshall Cavendish Corporation
2415 Jerusalem Avenue
North Bellmore, New York 11710
USA

© 1994 Marshall Cavendish Corporation

All rights reserved. No part of this book may be reproduced or utilized in
any form or by any means electronic or mechanical, including
photocopying, recording, or by any information storage and retrieval
system, without permission from the copyright holders.

Library of Congress Cataloging-in-Publication Data
Barden, Renardo.
    Juvenile violence / by Renardo Barden.
      p. cm. — (Life Issues)
    Includes bibliographical references and index.
    Summary: Examines the causes of juvenile violence at home,
in school, and on the streets and suggests alternatives and solutions.
    ISBN 1-85435-613-5:
    1. Juvenile delinquency—United States—Juvenile literature.
  2. Violence in children—United States—Juvenile literature.
  3. Family violence—United States—Juvenile literature.
  [1. Juvenile delinquency. 2. Violence. 3. Family violence.]
  I. Title. II. Series.
  HV9104.A5B343 1993   93-21656
  304.3'6'0973—dc20   CIP
                                        AC

Produced by The Creative Spark
Editor: Gregory Lee
Art direction: Robert Court
Design: Mary Francis-DeMarois, Robert Court
Page layout, graphic illustration: Elayne Roberts

Marshall Cavendish Editorial director: Evelyn M. Fazio
Marshall Cavendish Editorial consultant: Marylee Knowlton

Printed and bound in the United States of America

Photographic Note
Several persons depicted in this book are photographic models; their appearance in these photographs is solely to
dramatize some of the situations and choices facing readers of the Life Issues series.

Photo Credits
Big Brothers/Big Sisters of America, 85
Christie Costanzo 16, 34, 52, 78, 88
Image Works 4 (Michael Siluk); 6, 63 (Alan Carey); 10 (Bob Kalman); 30 (Carl Glassman); 40, 66 (B. Bachman)
Impact Visuals 42 (Andrew Lichtenstein)
Outward Bound 83 (Joseph Bailey)
PhotoEdit 13, 54, 72 (Michael Newman); 18, 24, 76 (Robert Brenner); 20, 80 (Mark Richards); 27, 56 (Tony Freeman);
36 (David Young-Wolff); 48 (CLEO); 59 (Phil McCarten); 69 (Richard Hutchings)

Cover photo: PhotoEdit (Elena Rooraid)

Acknowledgments
Thanks to Lt. Frank Messar, Executive Officer, Youth Services Division, Yonkers Police Department, for reviewing this manuscript.

3 9510 2002 3908 8

TABLE OF CONTENTS

PROLOGUE

T his book is for and about you and people like you—people who have witnessed, experienced, or are afraid of juvenile violence. It describes some of the efforts being put forth every day to make the world a little safer from violence. It is also about some of the actions you personally may need to take in order to survive, prosper, and live a less violent life.

Is life for young people in the United States more violent today than ever before? Yes. In the last 15 years juvenile violence has skyrocketed. In 1981, one in every ten people arrested for murder was under 18. By 1990 it was one in six.

While experts argue about why these numbers have jumped so dramatically in recent years, there is a shortage of information about how to avoid becoming a statistic—and survive this violent phase of American life.

When people are afraid, they tend to be extremely critical of themselves. They may conclude that they are cowards. If they are convinced that they are bad, they may even think they have brought violence on themselves—that they deserved it. This is not true. No one deserves to be subjected to violence.

If you are afraid of juvenile violence, you need to know that fear is not necessarily a sign of weakness or cowardice. Like pain, fear is a valuable signal. If you're sick, you should go to the doctor. If you're afraid, you should take action by dealing with or removing yourself from dangerous circumstances.

The danger of fear is that it can be paralyzing. You must not allow fear to prevent you from taking action to improve your circumstances. You must avoid dwelling on your fears by concentrating on your creative energies. By reading this book you have taken a positive first step toward creating change in your life. Now, you must learn to take positive action for your own good and for the good of others.

1

VIOLENCE BEGINS AT HOME

When I was small I used to think I must be a bad person to make my dad mad and hit me like that.
—Jeffrey, age 15

Geri, age 14, hurried home from school. Because she had gotten a late start that morning, she hadn't taken time to eat breakfast. She went into the kitchen and looked for something to eat. Disappointed that there wasn't much to snack on, she went to check on her brothers. Her eight-year-old brother Michael and her five-year-old brother Ben were watching television in the family room.

"Where's mom?" she asked Michael.

"She went to the bank," Michael said. "You're supposed to babysit." Geri noticed that Ben's toys were all over the floor.

"Ben," she said, realizing her mom would hold her responsible for the mess, "pick up your toys."

"I don't want to."

"I didn't ask if you wanted to," Geri shouted. "Get over there and pick up your toys or I'll break them!"

"No!" Ben yelled.

Geri swatted Ben sharply on the bottom. "I said pick up those toys." The swat made Ben more defiant. He picked up a GI Joe figure and threw it at her. The toy sailed past her face. She stomped it to pieces.

"I told you to listen. Now pick up the others before I smash them, too."

Fights between siblings are not unusual, but if physical violence is repeatedly tolerated in the home, children may think that violence is the right way to solve problems.

Ben cried over the broken figure, but he began picking up the toys and putting them away. Michael was laughing at Ben, fueling the small boy's anger. Geri went back to the kitchen for a glass of milk. Before she could return, she heard Ben wail with pain and start to cry again.

"What did you do to him?" she demanded of Michael.

"Nothing," Michael said.

"He pushed me against the wall," Ben told Geri.

"I didn't, either. I just shoved him because he was in front of the TV screen and I couldn't see. He fell down and went boom." Michael thought this was funny and started to laugh.

At that moment, their mother came in the back door and heard Ben's bawling. Ben, still crying, pointed a finger at Michael. Without saying a word, the mother whacked Michael across the face.

"I told you a hundred times not to make him cry," she yelled. Michael fought back tears and tried to explain, but his mother had already left the room.

"I'll get you later, you big baby," Michael told Ben.

FAMILY VIOLENCE

Many children and teenagers live in homes where people tend to hit first and ask questions later. Deep down, Geri, Michael, Ben, and their mother care about one another, but they have accepted and make use of practices that are harmful. Using physical violence is a little like trying to drive a nail with a screwdriver. Sometimes it works, but it is not the most effective way to do it. Physical violence may bring some action to a halt, but it does not fundamentally change unwanted or annoying behavior. Each member of this family uses physical violence as if it were a tool to shape the behavior of others.

- Geri swatted Ben, using violence to obtain obedience.
- Ben threw his toy at Geri, using violence to express rage and frustration.
- Geri smashed the toy, using violence to punish.
- Michael pushed Ben down, using violence to obtain a desired behavior.
- The mother smacked Michael in the face, using violence to remedy violence.
- Michael threatened Ben with future violence. More than the other instances, that last one—Michael's threat—shows the futility of trying to stop violence with more violence. The mother may believe she is protecting Ben from Michael's bullying, but in reality, she is setting the stage for future violence.

While there is disagreement about many things in the study of human behavior, experts tend to agree on one thing: Whether a violent event takes place in a shopping mall, on a dark street, in a school yard, or even in another country, violence generally begins at home.

IS VIOLENCE TAUGHT?

By using our ability to imitate others, we learn to stand, walk, run, talk, and interact with others. In the process, we discover that what we need and want produces conflict when our needs run counter to those around us. A baby, for example, may want to be comforted by its mother, while the mother may want to rest by watching television. Fundamental to the parent/child relationship is the word "no." A child soon learns that disregarding "no" may lead to violence.

Most of us first experience both human love and human abuse in our own home. One expert, Murray A. Straus, author of *Behind Closed Doors: Violence in the American Family*, believes that as babies and children we feel anger and resentment toward those who hit us. At the same time, our need to believe in our caregivers is so great that we learn to accept physical punishment as being intended for our own good. We learn to equate caring and love with violence, and to accept it as natural behavior. When people brought up in this way become parents, they continue to believe in the moral rightness of physical punishment, and will use it on their own children. In this way, the circle of family violence is complete. Ultimately, no family member is immune to violence.

In American families, spouse abuse (most commonly, abuse of the mother by the father) occurs in 16 percent of all households. Children attack their parents with similar frequency in about one out of six families. More common still are families where children receive violent treatment. Parents physically discipline their children in more than 63 percent of households. Physical fights between siblings occur in 80 percent of families having more than one child.

Fifty years ago, most people tended to believe that spanking and physical punishment were useful in the raising of children. Today, few experts endorse physical punishment. Why? Because research has established a strong connection between those who were violently disciplined as children and those who have served prison sentences for violent crimes.

Of course, not everyone who was spanked by his or her parents turns into a thug; not every boy who hits his sister turns into a rapist. But just because some people who were physically punished as children are doing well in life does not mean physical punishment is healthy.

WHY DO PARENTS SPANK AND HIT?

If parents use physical punishment, it does not mean they are bad or ignorant. Perhaps they are traditionalists—obeying unwritten rules their parents taught them. They may believe, as people in some cultures do, that hitting children is the proper way to make them obedient. The phrase "spare the rod and spoil the child" is a saying more than 1,000 years old.

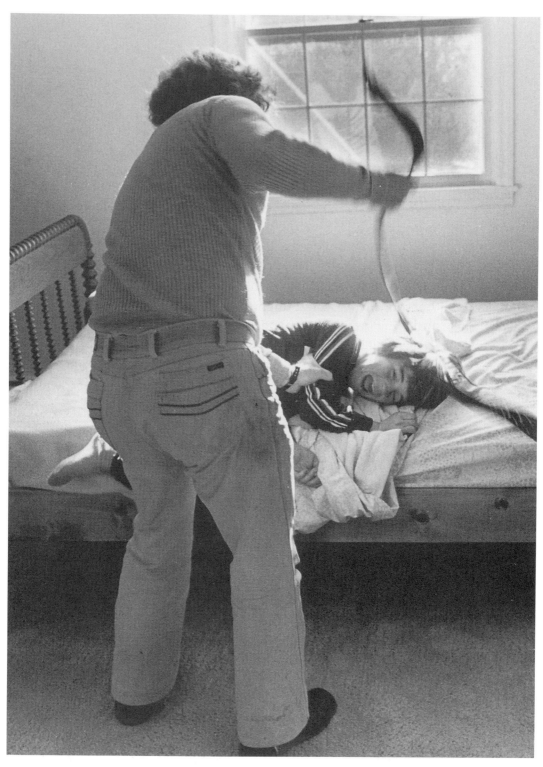

Spanking is a common method used by parents to discipline a child. Unfortunately, too many parents cross the line and inflict beatings that can lead to serious injuries.

Human beings learn to change many of their traditionally held views over time. Consider this example: In the Middle Ages, it was common to cover the bodies of sick people with blood-sucking leeches. This practice weakened and often killed the patients when perhaps all that was needed was nourishment and rest.

Parents sometimes spank because they can't think of any other way to express their frustrations. A parent discovers that a swat on the bottom will have an immediate effect on a child's behavior and not require a lot of words. A small boy may not stop beating on a pan with a spoon the first time he's asked, but he will almost certainly stop if he is grabbed by the arm and struck on the backside with the spoon. Apart from stopping the behavior, however, such an action is likely to have a secondary effect; it can produce anger and resentment that may be expressed later as violence against another person. Much of the time it is expressed again and again when these children grow up and have children of their own.

Juan is one such example. He is 27 and his wife Eve is 31. Juan has had a drug problem in the past, a problem he knows he still has to fight every day. When Eve lost her job, she collected unemployment. When her unemployment ran out, they and their newly born son Jason were forced to live on Juan's small salary. Things were bad, and tempers flared. Juan started beating Eve. The neighbors called the police.

"They saw me, they saw her black eye, they said they had to arrest me," said Juan. "My son was screaming. He was only a month old, but he knew something was wrong. I was having a flashback to my father beating my mother. My father's changed, but he used to come home and my mother would have dinner and he'd smash it on the floor and she'd have to make it all over again to keep peace. Once my father hit my mother and I ran across the room to stop it. He picked me up and threw me against the refrigerator and I passed out. I thought if I don't stop, the same will happen to Jason. He'll beat girls, too." Juan realized he was becoming just like his father.

DRUGS, POVERTY, AND VIOLENCE

F rederick is in the fifth grade and likes school. What he doesn't like is going home after school and finding no one in the apartment and nothing to eat. Occasionally, he finds his mother Leanne home and in a good mood. She offers him ice cream, steak, fries, and all his favorite foods. Unfortunately, on other occasions he finds strangers there, smoking crack cocaine and partying. On those occasions, Leanne can be high and violent. Once she threw a frying pan at Frederick and hit him in the shoulder, just missing his head.

Drug and alcohol abuse are some of the leading causes of family violence and child abuse. Between 50 and 67 percent of all episodes of family abuse occur in households in which one or more members heavily abuse alcohol or drugs.

Why do so many of today's adults abuse alcohol and drugs? Many parents grew up when the economic picture was bright and promising. They looked forward to having families of their own and a lifestyle where they could afford good housing, plentiful food, expert medical care, and enjoyable vacations. Today's tough economic times, however, have made it hard for many parents to achieve "the good life." Where the household budget is under strain, it is common to find condtions ripe for family violence. The Child Abuse Registry, a hotline in Orange County, California, confirms that phone calls and reports of abuse rise 25 to 30 percent just before and after the annual April 15 tax filing deadline, a period of high stress when many people find they owe money to the government.

THE IMPACT OF LOW SELF-ESTEEM

Do you think of yourself as a good person? Do others like and admire you? Do you feel loved? Do you believe that you can be successful? Are you smart enough to accomplish what you want to accomplish?

These are important questions that concern us all at one time or another. How we answer them is a reflection of our self-esteem. Self-esteem is the capacity to respect and admire ourselves in a healthy and realistic way. Although we don't often tell friends how we "really" feel about ourselves, each of us senses the importance of such feelings.

Have you ever solved a hard math problem? When you got the right answer you probably felt a sense of well being, a surge of belief in yourself. You might have even felt, just for a moment, that you could do absolutely anything. The feelings of satisfaction that accompany personal successes—both big and small— reflect a healthy sense of self-esteem.

Have you ever flunked or done poorly on a test in school? How did you feel afterward? Did you feel that you were stupid, that the world was a dull and demanding place, that you were going to have a bad or disappointing future? Did you even feel ugly? Did your friends seem cold and aloof? Such feelings often signal low self-esteem.

THE VICIOUS CYCLE OF DRUGS AND ALCOHOL

One way people compensate for feelings of low self-esteem is through drug and alcohol abuse. Taking drugs and drinking alcohol produce a "high" that resembles a temporary boost in self-esteem, but it does not solve anyone's problems. In fact, the opposite is true. Substance abuse causes a new set of problems. People with low self-esteem are often attracted to drugs and alcohol because they provide a distraction from deep and painful problems that are tough to solve. One of the problems with drugs and alcohol is that after the high wears off, the low self-esteem returns, creating further need to escape the bad feelings through more drug and alcohol use. This creates a cycle of dependency that makes the substance abuser keep trying to boost his or her self-esteem with new highs.

People with high self-esteem do better at ordinary life tasks than those with low self-esteem. People with good self-esteem can better deal with failure because their greater sense of self-worth will see them through minor disappointments. But to people with low self-esteem, even minor disappointments can be upsetting.

If children are battered or abandoned by their parents, they will begin to feel insecure and unloved. Believing they are unable to sustain their parents' love and protection, they come to feel unworthy of parental love and experience a lowering of self-esteem. All children experience some disappointment and loss of self-esteem early in life. However, those whose needs are consistently not met develop profound self-esteem losses that cannot easily be repaired. Feelings of self-esteem, whether good or bad, are already deeply formed by the time children are three years old.

To compensate for low self-esteem as well as to make up for their lack of parental security, some kids join gangs. The gang gives them a purpose in life, takes the place of the family and, in effect, allows them to raise their self-esteem. Often, unable to raise their own low self-esteem, they seek to lower the self-esteem of others. They may turn to various put-downs, trying to rise by making others hit bottom. The extremes of such behavior are expressed through bullying, fighting, and other violent behavior.

Many youths with poor self-esteem and troubled home lives end up venting their anger and frustration through minor crimes or by joining gangs.

A DEATH IN THE FAMILY

When he was five, Mark made the mistake of telling his father that he was afraid of the dark. His father's response was to handcuff the small boy in the basement and leave him alone in the dark for hours. A few years later, he held the boy's hand over a red hot burner to punish him. When Mark was 15, his father stuck a gun in his son's mouth and threatened to shoot him. When he was 16, Mark was beaten, his head slammed into a radiator, and hit on the head with a hammer. During this beating, Mark managed to get a gun and shoot his father to death.

Under the circumstances, Mark's shooting of his father was ruled to be self-defense. When authorities learned what he had suffered at the hands of his father, Mark was able to avoid serious punishment. He was sentenced instead to six months probation.

"It may sound sick, but I did love him," Mark said. "I still love him. I mean, he was my father."

This reaction is not unusual. As psychologist and attorney Charles Patrick Ewing says, "We take the commandment to 'honor thy father and mother' very seriously. The implication is that you're supposed to honor your parents even if they abuse you."

An estimated 2.7 million youngsters were abused physically, mentally, or sexually by parents in 1991, according to the National Center for the Prevention of Child Abuse. Given these grim statistics, it may seem remarkable that the killing of a parent is so rare. The murder of a parent accounts for only about two percent of all homicides. Not surprisingly, most of the young people who killed one or more parents suffered from child abuse. In contrast, well over 1,000 parents killed children, often by beatings administered when the parent was high on drugs or alcohol. It is difficult to know for sure how many parents kill their children, because parents often pass off death or serious injuries to their children as the result of "falls" and other household accidents.

SHAME

Healthy families flourish under conditions of love, respect, and communication. Unhealthy families seem to be characterized by fear, silence, secrecy, and shame. If your family situation is destructive, shame will probably be one of the biggest obstacles you have to face in your search for a better life.

Rudy's and Terry's father was generous and occasionally brought them gifts and sat up watching TV late with them. But trouble started whenever he was drinking. Half-drunk, he would wander around the house looking for dirty dishes or missing tools. When he found something, he'd yank his sons out of bed, accuse them of wrecking his home, and beat them.

If their mother tried to stop the beatings, she would also be hit. One night when she poured his rum down the kitchen sink, he beat her until she was nearly unconscious. In the morning, Rudy and Terry skipped school and went instead to the nearest police station where they talked to a detective about their family problems.

That evening, two sheriffs came to the boys' house. While one waited for the father to come home, the other drove Rudy, Terry, and their mother to the hospital. The father was arrested. The mother filed charges against him and he was obliged to live apart from his family and get help with his drinking problem.

Although their father still has not returned to live with the family, the four of them are in therapy together. The brothers know that people gossip about them in the small town where they live, but Rudy and Terry agree that a little embarrassment and shame are better than the violence that was destroying them. As Terry puts it, "I'd much rather be a little embarrassed than be worried about my brother and mother. I'd rather hear people whispering behind my back than go to school still sore from a beating."

IF THERE IS VIOLENCE AT HOME

If you are physically attacked at home and are in danger of being injured or killed, you obviously must protect yourself, even when your attacker is a family member. But it is important to recognize the difference between self-defense and violence, and still more important to control your anger so that it does not lead to more violence. There is more to self-defense than exchanging slaps or punches. The best self-defense is not combat, but realistic and intelligent planning in advance of violent events.

If you are being abused at home, you must defend yourself by taking action immediately, before matters become worse. Physical violence and abuse always get worse when nothing is done about them. To some, just facing the problem is overwhelming, but taking any action toward a solution is a step in the right direction.

Begin by believing in yourself. It's very hard to value yourself when those around you do not, but remember that nobody deserves physical abuse. No matter how small you are or how worthless you've been made to feel, you are a unique being, capable of loving and deserve to be loved. To do this you must take care of yourself. If you are being abused, it does not mean you are unworthy of love and consideration; it means that the people you live with are incapable of valuing you. It is their problem, not yours. No one has the right to harm another human being—not even a family member.

Nothing you could do justifies your being beaten and abused. In most abusive families there are times of crisis when things get hot, followed by intervals of calm when things can seem almost normal. It is most often during times of crisis that abused people reach out for help. During the so-called "normal" times, people often hope against hope that things will improve. You must not let the "normal" times overcome your understandable fear.

However, it's one thing to tell yourself that you don't deserve abuse and another to actually avoid it. The first step is to stop feeling helpless.

DURING THE CRISIS

I f you're dealing with a crisis right now, if you or someone else in your family is being badly beaten or threatened with bodily injury, don't hesitate to do what thousands of other young people do every year: Seek safety outside the home. If you have recently escaped from violence and are scared to return home, go to the nearest police precinct and explain your situation. It is possible that the police or a social service agency will be able to help you improve your family situation. While you are still afraid and in danger, they may be able to help you find a place to stay—temporarily if things can be straightened out, permanently if not.

Telephone books have special sections that list frequently called numbers and include community service listings for people who need to talk to a hotline counselor about violence. Look under "Social Service Organizations" in the yellow pages.

In the back of this book you'll find a list of toll-free 800 numbers. Call as many of these numbers as you need to until you find someone you're comfortable talking to. Tell them everything that has been happening to you and that you want a place to go where you will be safe.

LEAVING HOME

W ith the help of a college scholarship and several social service agencies near her home, 18-year-old Hester is attending a school more than 1,000 miles from the town where she grew up.

"My dad and mom are alcoholics and use cocaine," she says. "They would get in horrible fights that often spilled over and involved me. Sometimes I'd get hit, or find my money stolen and my stereo hocked for drug money. Sometimes I'd get locked out. At times, they would both get clean at the same time and try to make things up to me. They'd start in a substance abuse program and I'd think, well, I love my parents. Things could be so good. But every time, one of them would try to sneak a drink or score a little coke and things would start to get bad again.

"I kept hoping for a long time that things would get better, but things only got better before a new period of getting worse. Each time things would start to go bad, I'd think I've got to seek some kind of help for myself. I've got to tell somebody what's going on in my 'happy home'...but I'd put it off. Then, one day my mom chased me down the street beating me with this huge umbrella. I ran to a friend's house and blurted my whole story out to him and his parents. They helped me out, referred me to a lot of different agencies, and though I've written my parents, I haven't been home since. Some day I'll probably see my parents again. But not until I've answered some questions for myself—like why I blamed myself for everything and why I waited so long to seek help. One of the things that held me back was shame over not having the family that people thought I had."

THE CALM BETWEEN CRISES

I f you are being abused at home, you must think of yourself first. You must take the actions necessary to get relief from your situation. Of course, it is likely that others in your household also face danger. During lulls between violent episodes, when you are not in immediate danger, consider other family members as well.

Who are the others being abused? Are they older or younger than you? If they are older, you must attempt to get through to them right away. Try and get their cooperation by letting them know that you love and care for them and are concerned about their safety. Talk to them and help them see that they are not to blame, that their behavior does not cause or contribute to the abuse. Let them know that help is available. Once you have won their loyalty and support, enlist them as helpers. The more support you can win from other family members, the better off you'll be when it comes time to act.

If you have younger brothers and sisters, you may not be able to get them to help you. Even so, you should let them know you love and care for them. Try to help them understand that their behavior does not cause the violence in the family. Tell them that you intend to do something to improve their circumstances.

If one of your parents is also being battered, you have a special challenge. You must try to communicate with them in a loving way and let them know that you are concerned for their health and safety. Unfortunately, parents are often more inclined to blame themselves instead of others for abuse in the family.

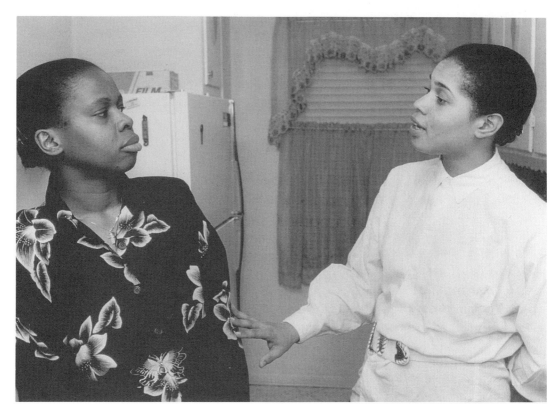

Often a spouse who is abused will protest and tell the children in the family to not "rock the boat." Abused spouses, however, need immediate help, whether they believe it or not.

If it is your mother who is being abused, she may not be willing to go up against your father. You may have to proceed without her support. Like Rudy's and Terry's mother, she may be even more afraid to seek help than you are. She may feel more shame and more fear, and may be inclined to believe that "things will get better." In an abusive situation, this is a false and dangerous belief. But don't judge her; seek help for her. If necessary, proceed without her knowledge. If she is willing to talk about the problem, tell her there are shelters for battered women, some of which accommodate children and young people. Again, seek help either with or without the support of your mother, brothers, or sisters.

Finally, after you are safe from harm, you will probably want to consider the plight of the abuser. If your family life is like the lives of other people who have grown up in abusive environments, you already know that the abuser is capable of love and remorse. Keep your sights set on self-help first, however, and don't let yourself be drawn back into a cycle of sympathy for the abuser. Things have gone too far. He or she needs help immediately. That help can only come from outside the abusive family in the form of intervention from someone he or she can't hit, kick, beat, molest, and then try to make it all better with kisses and presents.

Timing is important. For example, don't try to discuss alcohol-related abuse with the abuser when he or she is drunk and running around the house breaking things. Be patient and watchful. When you discuss these subjects, you will have to do it in a way that the abuser does not find threatening. The idea is to make yourself a helpful source of information to the abuser.

One of the hotlines you'll find in this book is for Parents Anonymous. These people are parents themselves, and they talk kindly to abusive parents in an effort to persuade them to get some help so that the family situation does not deteriorate further. In addition, Parents Anonymous may be able to refer your parents to local groups of parents who meet regularly in an effort to manage their anger and frustration. Perhaps you could arrange to have one of them speak with your abusive parent.

Friends are always important, but people from abusive families have a special need for friendship and goodwill. If you're in an abusive situation at home, you must avoid isolation. Stay close with your friends and don't be afraid to make new friends. More than a few battered and abused juveniles have found in friends and their friends' parents the love and respect they can't count on at home. Teachers, school nurses, and social service case workers can also be helpful.

2

GROWING UP VIOLENT

Would I change anything at home?
Maybe have a father around.
—Juan, age 15

Clyde, 17, and his brother Gary, 14, get along very well. Not long ago, their mother Karen lost her job. The family had to move from a pleasant high-rise to a smaller, older apartment in a tough neighborhood.

With family income down and Clyde's need for money increasing, he decided to look for a part-time job. A week after moving into the new apartment, Clyde hit the streets with a resume he'd written on his computer.

When it got dark and Clyde failed to come home, Karen and Gary went looking for him. They found him walking home. His face was bruised and cut, his shirt was torn, and one of his front teeth had been knocked out. He had been beaten by a neighborhood street gang and robbed of the five dollars he had in his pocket. Karen and Gary took him to an emergency room where he was treated and released. Gary cried when he saw how badly Clyde had been beaten.

Clyde was a victim of juvenile violence, and—indirectly—so were his mother and brother. Karen had to come up with $500 for Clyde's dental work and fell behind on other family expenses. Gary, now in therapy for nightmares, is afraid to go out of the house by himself.

Neighborhood gangs—often identified by their hand signs and clothing—create many problems for other young people who just want to be free to go to school and to a playground without being threatened.

"For a long time after Clyde got beat up," Gary admits, "I used to have night-mares about both of us getting jumped. During the day, instead of paying attention to what was going on in school, I'd be daydreaming about going out for revenge against the guys who hurt Clyde. I'm better now, but for a while there, Clyde's getting beat up started to take over my whole life. I had trouble thinking about anything else." Sadly, another reason that kids join gangs is precisely to gain protection from the kind of scare that Clyde and Gary had.

After Clyde was attacked, a neighborhood newspaper wrote about it as "another episode of senseless juvenile violence." Clyde wrote a letter to the edtor objecting to the phrase "senseless violence."

"It wasn't 'senseless,'" Clyde wrote. "They saw me getting change for a five-dollar bill. They were thieves who wanted my money, and they were willing to beat me up, injure, or even kill me for it. That's cold-blooded, but it's not senseless."

VIOLENCE COMES IN MANY FORMS

The law defines a juvenile as an individual age 18 or under and not fully responsible for his or her actions (some states have narrowed this definition to anyone over age seven and under age 16). Defining violence is not nearly as simple. Which of the following incidents do you think are violent?

- A baby girl who dislikes having her face wiped waves her arms at her mother. The mother yanks the girl's hair and swipes her chin with a damp paper napkin.
- A small boy in a grocery cart reaches for a supermarket shelf and yells for cookies. His mother, annoyed, slaps his arm.
- In the school cafeteria, the bigger Brian pushes the smaller Glen from the line and takes his place.
- In front of school, Sharisse hits Lynette for calling her a name.
- An older boy who doesn't attend school punches Gordon and demands his lunch money.
- Jason and Adam call each other names. Adam slugs Jason. A circle of kids gather around clamoring for a fight.
- When Shelly visits a friend, she hears a family quarrel coming from an apartment on the second floor. She hears bad language and what sounds like a child crying.
- Ken wakes up in the middle of a summer night to the sound of voices screaming obscenities in the street.
- Eileen hears what sound like gunshots. Moments later the wail of a siren fills the street.
- In a shopping center parking lot, Michele heard a boy shouting at his younger sister, "You're a worthless pig!"

The first six incidents are obviously violent. But how about the last four? There's very little information to make an accurate judgment, but they are violent because they involve harm or the intent to harm others. They are violent because—at the very least—they harm the self-esteem and feelings of the witnesses.

In fact, when we consider the impact of name-calling on a person's self-esteem, aren't all these episodes violent? The famous saying, "Sticks and stones may break my bones, but names will never hurt me," represents an effort not to be hurt by name-calling episodes. But does it really work? Have you ever been hurt by something someone said to you? Did it affect you after the incident was over? To keep it from affecting you, did you have to persuade yourself that the person who called you a name was unimportant? Did it cause you to hate that person, or to want to hurt him or her? Unfortunately, many kids grow up in homes and neighborhoods where these examples are not thought of as violent, but instead as merely routine—a regular part of life.

Professional athletes often claim that their "mental preparation" is as important to their success as physical conditioning. They believe that thoughts and feelings, often described as "attitude," are very much a part of who they are and how they perceive themselves. It is true that attitude does affect how people perform various tasks, including how they handle the aggressive behavior of others and themselves.

VIOLENCE OR AGGRESSION?

One warm spring afternoon, Derek went on a picnic with his class in a city park. After eating, the class wandered down to a nearby lake. At first, most of the students started "skipping" flat stones on the water. Then a couple of girls took off their shoes to put their feet in the water. Some of the boys took off their shoes and socks and waded into the lake. Before long, Derek joined them.

Derek had a crush on Ginger and tried several times to splash her. Finally frustrated, he picked her up and carried her out into the water. Ginger told him several times to put her down. Two of Ginger's girlfriends tried to stop him, but Derek persisted and dropped Ginger into the water. She fell on a sharp stone and cut her leg. The cut was not deep, but it was painful and made her cry. One of Ginger's friends told their teacher later, "Derek got violent and threw Ginger into the water." Derek apologized and admitted that he'd been too aggressive, but denied that he'd been violent.

When is an act "aggressive" and when is it "violent?" On the football field, tackling is part of the game and is not considered an act of violence. On the dance floor where it is not expected, tackling is considered violent. Violence is inappropriate aggressive behavior that results in physical harm to someone else.

Injuring or attempting to injure others, except in self-defense, is always violence. Derek was violent with Ginger; it is always violent to force another person to do something they do not wish to do.

THE VIOLENT GENDER?

G inger went home and asked her parents a question. "Why is it that whenever somebody gets hurt, there's always a guy involved?"

"Men, by and large, tend to act outwards and be more aggressive," says Ronald Ebert, a psychologist at McLean's Hospital in Belmont, Massachusetts. "Girls tend to internalize pain and blame themselves more." Although male children tend to respond differently to conditions of stress and violence, most authorities on child behavior tend to agree that males are more likely to be aggressive or use force or violence to solve problems or get what they want. (Nevertheless, more cities than ever are reporting that females are becoming more violent, committing more vicious assaults as well as becoming gang members.)

The FBI reported in 1990 that 82 percent of all suspects arrested nation-wide are male, that 89 percent of all violent crimes that result in arrests are commited by males, and that males are more likely to be the victims of murder by more than 2-to-1.

Men and boys are generally regarded as more aggressive than women and girls. Boys who play too rough without realizing it may become more violent as they grow older.

All this has stimulated scientific interest in testosterone, the male sex hormone. Testosterone affects the male prostate gland, contributes to greater muscle mass, deepens the voice, and stimulates the growth of body hair. For that reason, testosterone is generally considered the "male" hormone.

Some experts dispute that males are born more aggressive and violent than females. They argue that not all people with high amounts of testosterone turn to violence. For now, there is no biological explanation for violence that is useful to anyone trying to avoid it.

ROLE MODELS

One Saturday, Shawn, Roland, and Damien took some water balloons to a freeway overpass after school. Thinking it would be fun to drop them on passing cars, they invited Roland's cousin Tyson to join them. At first, Tyson thought the idea was funny and decided to go along with the scheme.

"Sometimes when you're bored with television and haven't had a good time for a while, the idea of doing almost anything different seems cool," he said. "But when I looked down at the cars on the highway, the idea didn't seem as funny. The thing is, unlike those other guys, I'd been in a car accident when I was eight. I wasn't injured, but my dad broke his wrist and got a cut on his face. When we got to the highway I realized that the water balloons might land on a car and cause an accident."

Tyson suggested that instead of throwing the water balloons at cars, they throw them at one another. When the others insisted on using them to bomb the traffic, Tyson went home. His friends dropped three or four balloons from the overpass before an off-duty fireman saw what they were doing and stopped his car.

"I couldn't see what they were dropping," Terry the fireman said, "but whatever it was, I knew it could cause a serious accident. It wasn't until after I got out and started yelling at them that I realized I knew the boys. Two years before, I'd worked with them as a counselor at the summer YMCA camp."

Rather than reporting them, Terry gave each of the boys a choice. They could call their mothers and tell them what they'd been doing, or they could ride with him to the nearby fire station. The boys chose the latter.

At the station, Terry and some of the other firemen showed the boys photographs of serious car accidents. The pictures were gruesome. In some of the accidents, the fire department had to use special equipment to free trapped passengers.

One of the firemen, Rich, belonged to an organization known as Big Brothers. He wasn't surprised to learn that none of the boys had a father or older brothers living at home. He told them a little about Big Brothers and how they team younger males with older males, allowing them to form strong friendships. Big Brothers spend regular time with their little brothers, providing the guidance that these young males need in place of the absent father. Roland and Damien said they wanted to enroll in the program, hoping to connect with an older male like Rich who would share some of his interests and be like an older brother.

FAMILIES WITHOUT FATHERS

T he traditional family, consisting of mother, father, and children all living together under one roof, is much less common today than at any time in American history. Divorce, having children without marrying, and the single-parent family have become as common in our society as the traditional two-parent family used to be. Increasingly, young people like Shawn, Roland, and Damien live with one rather than two parents. That parent is usually their mother.

Since males generally learn "male" behavior from their fathers, single-parent households often have special problems. When the mother is taking care of female children, role modeling presents no problem and girls are able to model themselves after their mothers. In cases where the child is a male living with his mother, however, the male child finds no one at home to pattern himself after. Of course, this doesn't mean all boys being raised by their mothers alone will get into trouble, but it makes it that much harder.

Criminologists have long observed a connection between violent criminal behavior and the lack of fathers or significant male role models in the lives of offenders. In one study, three scientists found that the lack of a father's influence tended to produce men who lacked empathy, which is the capacity to identify with and feel what others feel.

Gary showed empathy by crying when his brother Clyde was beaten. Tyson showed empathy in not bombarding cars with water balloons. People with empathy are unlikely to hurt an animal, spank a child, steal from others, shoot at a person they don't like, or commit other violent acts. In contrast, those lacking in empathy do not think about the feelings of others, and they are more inclined to act without regard to the feelings of others—sometimes violently. When Derek threw Ginger in the water, more than a dozen other boys did not behave that way. Who had more empathy?

Some research suggests that small boys may blame their mother for the absence of a father, even when the mother is not to blame. In male children, this can result in feelings of hostility toward the mother and, eventually, toward all females. Feelings of anger and blame may prevent some young males from developing a strong sense of empathy—especially for girls and women. This lack encourages them to do whatever they want to others without thinking of the consequences.

The lack of a father in a boy's life is often cited as a reason some males behave more violently than others.

The fireman who stopped the boys from throwing the water balloons did not believe the boys were mean or evil. Like many others who get in trouble, they simply did not stop to consider what could happen. They did not think before they acted. "Bombing the cars with those balloons seemed like it would be totally cool," Damien recalls now. "Sometimes it seems like a lot of adults just don't want to see anybody having more fun than them. But seeing those pictures—I guess they made us think...A driver could lose control when the balloon hit. To tell you the truth, I'm glad we got caught. The last thing I want to live with is knowing I made somebody get hurt or killed."

AN EMOTIONAL PRISON

For as long as he could remember, Martin's grandfather did everything with him: Taught him how to play baseball, took him fishing, bought him a bike, fixed his broken toys, took him shopping, and told him stories about life when he was a boy. As he grew older, however, Martin started hanging out with groups of kids in the neighborhood and didn't see his grandfather as often. Then the old man got sick and Martin saw even less of him. One night the phone rang. When Martin answered it, his grandmother was crying. His grandfather had just died. Martin's mother and sisters all started crying, but Martin just went to his room and acted like he didn't care.

At the funeral, relatives attempting to pray out loud in church started to cry and couldn't finish. The only dry-eyed person there was Martin. He nodded to his friends but didn't really talk to them. He ignored his family.

A week after the funeral, Martin's friend Davis asked Martin a question in their chemistry class. When Martin ignored him, Davis asked if he was deaf. Martin suddenly became angry. He pushed the table over and started hitting Davis. He was sent to the principal's office, and his mother was called. His mother started crying and scolded him over the phone because she had to leave work and pick him up from school. When Martin hung up, he got out of his chair and punched the wall so hard that he broke his hand. He was suspended from school.

In order to be readmitted, Martin had to agree to counseling. After a couple of sessions, the therapist told Martin's mother that Martin didn't want to talk about his feelings. He said that Martin's fight and punching the wall were really expressions of grief over the death of his grandfather. His mother tried to understand, but said she was worried because Martin didn't come home much anymore and had become so "macho."

THE CODE OF MACHO

The word *macho* is of Latin origin, and is used by Spanish-speaking people to refer to a style of masculine behavior characterized by virility, physical courage, and aggressiveness. In popular American culture, the term often applies to behavior that seems masculine in the extreme—exaggerated and phony.

Following the code of macho means restricting one's emotions. Tears and crying are forbidden to those who follow a macho code. In fact, the macho code is a kind of emotional prison in which many men and boys choose to live. If the only emotion a man allows himself to show is anger, then he is going to have to express a lot of anger. Because it is concerned with power and control over others, macho behavior limits the freedom of others as well. Since anger is one of the few allowable emotions, anger becomes the staple of a macho man's emotional life. Worse, it can become the force that torments wives, children, and other males.

Why do males get caught up in macho behavior? For one thing, they are strongly motivated to seek the approval of other males. According to child development specialists, boys at certain ages would rather have the approval of other males than the admiration of females. Macho behavior is a way of expressing solidarity or unity with other males. While it is socially permissible for females to hug and kiss and relate freely to other females, such physical affection is socially forbidden to males. Young boys sense early on that if they want the admiration and respect of other boys, they will have to learn to express themselves through macho rituals that older males can accept.

THE MACHO MYSTIQUE

Faced with the uncertainties of manhood, many young males adopt a macho attitude. Macho is a code, a definition of maleness that defines how "a man" ought to act. Among its characteristics are:

Anger. It's okay to be angry and to make a show of expressing anger. Revenge is one acceptable expression of anger. But most other emotions are out of bounds (except for sulking or pouting).

Stoicism. Whatever you do, don't show "excessive" emotion. Don't express pleasure, sorrow, grief, or happiness. Above all, don't admit that you feel pain, cry, or show emotions. Don't express affection, except in male-approved ways like "high fives."

Strength. Be strong and unyielding. Take a stand and never abandon it, even if that stand turns out to be wrong or appears to be unworkable. Don't ask for help.

Show your contempt for weakness. Let other guys know when you think they're acting like "wimps." Let your girlfriend and other females around you know that you don't approve of emotional displays.

Be in control. Don't let anybody tell you what to do or think. Don't let your girlfriend push you around. Be the boss.

The most macho kids in gangs are sometimes called "gangsters." They are the ones who pull the trigger during a shooting.

3

VIOLENCE IN SCHOOL

School isn't fun when you have security guards around.
—Tina, age 16

Jeff is macho, is bigger than any of the other boys in class, has trouble reading and doing his schoolwork, and likes to fight. Lincoln is small, does well in school, and is the class clown. In the schoolyard, Jeff slapped and pushed Lincoln and challenged him to a fight. Although Lincoln tried to make a joke of it, Jeff's friend Ricky said Lincoln was actually making fun of Jeff and goaded him to hit Lincoln in the mouth. Jeff slugged Lincoln, and although Lincoln fought back, he ended up with a black eye, a bloody nose, and tears streaming down his face.

Jill knows all three boys. She thinks Lincoln is the cutest guy in school. She doesn't care much for Jeff because he seems to have an attitude problem. Ricky, the boy who egged Jeff on, has a crush on Jill. She doesn't dislike Ricky, but she finds the way he behaves a little embarrassing. It's also hard for her to understand why Jeff lets himself be controlled by Ricky.

BULLIES

Jeff fits the classic profile of a bully. What's interesting about bullies, both male and female, is that they are all very much alike and tend to have very similar personality traits.

Bullies in school are not new. They pick on people they know they can humiliate.

- They tend to be larger and stronger than the people who fear them.
- They tend to have low self-esteem and do poorly in school. Since they have a low opinion of themselves, bullies enjoy lowering the self-esteem of others. If a bully is in school at all, chances are he or she is doing poorly.
- Although they pretend to enjoy conflict, bullies tend to only pick fights that they're sure to win.
- They delight in bringing out cowardly behavior in others. Lincoln's attempt to joke and make a show of friendship toward Jeff was ineffective.

HOW TO HANDLE A BULLY

If there's a bully in your life, you've probably already scolded yourself for being a coward. But getting down on yourself only makes things more difficult. It is important to be perfectly honest with yourself. Others have survived the experience of being afraid and so will you.

Make a list of the things that you're most afraid the bully might do. After a day or two, look at the list again. This time, reorganize it so that those things the bully is most likely to do are on the top. Now think of your list as a series of problems for which there might be solutions.

If you think the bully is likely to demand your lunch money, maybe you can have your parents arrange to pay for it in advance by check. Is the bully likely to punch you? Try to stay a little later in class, or be the first to leave the room. Can you sit where you are less visible, transfer to another class, or change your routines?

Granted, these are just strategies for avoiding the bully. If someone is really after you, he or she may not be so easy to avoid. Even so, avoidance can work to your advantage. Most of us don't plan well when we're under stress. Think of avoiding the bully as a way to have a breather that will let you come up with a more permanent and workable solution to the bully problem. You may not have to avoid him or her for very long before other targets are found.

Ask yourself why this bully persecutes you. If you can understand the bully's motives, you may think of things to say and do that will make you a less desirable victim. For example, if the bully enjoys humiliating you in front of others, find out why he or she craves the admiration of those you hang out with. Once you find out who the bully admires so much, perhaps that person can be recruited to persuade the bully to leave you alone.

Experiment with other attitudes toward the bully that make you less vulnerable. If the bully seems to delight in making you feel afraid, summon up your courage and try to respond less dramatically. If it's possible to talk with the bully, you may be able to learn more about what makes him or her tick. Maybe you've done something offensive. If so, try to straighten things out or apologize—but without groveling. An apology should not make the bully want to humiliate you.

Unfortunately, bullies frequently ignore apologies and seek only the pain and suffering of their victims. If the problem is serious and you think the bully is armed with a gun or a knife, it is a good idea to consult a teacher, counselor, principal, parent, older brother, advisor, school security guard, or another responsible adult. You shouldn't have to confront a dangerous situation—don't be afraid to ask for help.

What about fighting back? Professional boxing, wrestling, and karate are organized into weight divisions for the logical reason that size is important in physical combat. If you're a person who is lightweight and small in stature, be realistic. You might get lucky, but you will not be successful fighting larger opponents. That's why there's no harm in avoiding or running from the bully. So you're not a fighter. You may make a great jockey, ballet dancer, or musician. Maybe your gift is singing, math, or repairing electronic equipment. To run away from a fight you can't win may seem cowardly—especially in the eyes of those with a taste for violent entertainment—but you don't owe the crowd entertainment. Instead, you owe yourself the safety and kindness you would like to show to others.

Certainly pride and self-respect are important and may be worth the risk and even the pain. But before you decide to fight back, you should find out something about the bully's habits. It has been estimated that as many as 100,000 students carried a gun to school in 1992, and no estimates were made about the number who carried knives. Do not, under any circumstances, provoke a person who may be armed.

WHAT DO STUDENTS WORRY ABOUT?

Percentage of high school seniors reporting their most pressing concerns:

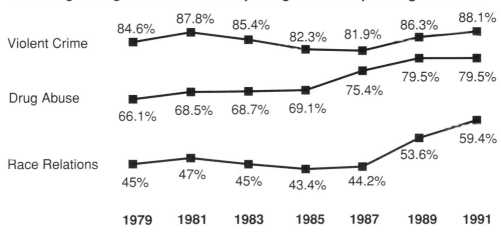

From: *Sourcebook of Criminal Justice Statistics, 1991: U.S. Department of Justice, Bureau of Justice Statistics.*

THE REST OF THE STORY

The morning after the fight between Jeff and Lincoln, Jill was walking out of geography class when she heard what sounded like firecrackers exploding in the hallway. There was a lot of commotion, and then Jill saw two police officers leading Lincoln out of school in handcuffs. Jill found out later that Lincoln had brought his father's pistol to school. He had told Jeff to get down on his knees and beg for his life, then he fired into the ceiling. The basketball coach had grabbed Lincoln and taken away the gun.

It's hard to find anything to admire about Jeff or Ricky or the kids who stood around when Lincoln got beat up, so it may be tempting to admire Lincoln. After all, he had to overcome his fears in order to stand up to Jeff. But it would be a mistake to think of him as heroic for bringing a gun to school. Guns are not solutions to violence and they certainly don't belong in school. Lincoln's most serious offense might be firing the gun, but he could easily have killed or wounded someone. Unfortunately, many kids bring guns to school for protection. They rarely use them, but having them in school automatically makes school more dangerous.

Lincoln was taken to a juvenile detention center where he had to enroll in a special program designed for young people who carried guns to school. Lincoln, Rick, and Jeff were made to see a school counselor to work out their problems. The guidance counselor listened to their versions of the events and noted that the word "dissed"—being putdown—occurred in each of them. Each boy wanted respect. Lincoln, Jeff, and Ricky all mentioned one or more things that made them feel like using violence:

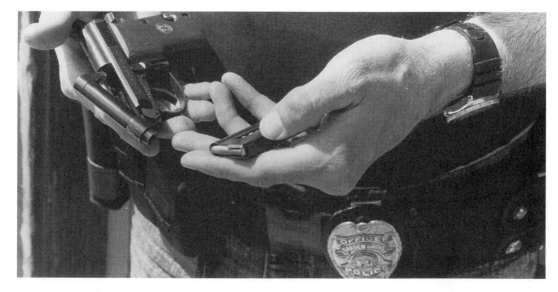

So many students are bringing guns to school that many schools are using metal detectors and full-time security officers to curb the problem.

- *Insults.* A deliberate show of disrespect for others is the leading cause of juvenile assaults in school and elsewhere. If you have been a victim of juvenile violence at school, the odds are very good that insulting behavior played a part in it. You can reduce your odds of being involved in violence by showing respect for others and not talking about people behind their backs. Sadly, the insult does not have to be real—it may only be in the other person's mind. Their reaction is what counts.
- *Rumors.* Sometimes things get a little slow at school. This often prompts students to exaggerate incidents or even make them up. You can reduce the amount of violence at school by downplaying rumors, ignoring them, and refusing to repeat them.
- *Rivalry.* If you have feelings of envy or jealousy, recognize them for what they are—feelings that anyone might have from time to time. Try to deal with them in an honest and realistic way. Trying to make others like and respect you by hurting someone else is not realistic and usually backfires.
- *Peer Pressure.* Do your friends seem to like and admire you when you behave violently or show your approval of violence? Do they withdraw their friendship when you do not do what they want? If so, then you already know what peer pressure is. You probably also realize that school life is made tougher than necessary by this kind of pressure.

Many of the most violent episodes that involve young people also involve peer pressure. Like bullies, peer pressure presents difficult problems. You probably won't be able to reform a bully's character, and you probably won't be able to banish peer pressure from your life. But you can reduce its impact if you're willing to take a look at your friends and ask yourself why you're friendly with them if their company always seems to get you in trouble. True friends don't encourage violence. Do your friends want what's best for you, or do they just want you to help them create a little excitement or free entertainment?

THE IMPACT OF GUNPLAY

A teacher's aide at a child care center noticed that a three-year-old boy had a large bulge in his coat pocket. On being asked about it, the boy produced what looked to be a toy pistol. However, a closer examination revealed that the gun was a .25-caliber pistol.

The little boy was taken to a nearby hospital for a checkup, and then turned over to authorities until his parents could be questioned. Asked where he got the gun, he told police he found the gun on the front seat of a van. A family friend had driven the boy to school and left the gun in plain sight on the seat. The child simply picked it up and put it in his coat pocket.

Young people are using guns on each other at an alarming rate. Usually the incidents are accidents, but three-fourths of all juvenile homicides are committed with guns.

While the above story from today's headlines is an extreme example, guns in school are no longer a rarity. Fist fights in the yard after school and brawls at high school basketball games have given way to gun flare-ups that too often end in death. As one young man in Detroit put it recently, "There are no more fights in Detroit. It's just guns now."

Many of these guns are bought from drug dealers or acquired in residential burglaries. Other guns are simply taken from the home. A Florida school study found that 86 percent of the guns taken from students were from their own homes. A recent survey of Baltimore public school students showed that 59 percent of the kids from single-parent or no-parent homes had carried handguns to school. The National School Safety Center estimated that 135,000 students carried guns to school in 1987.

In a suburban school outside Boston, a teacher asked a group of kids, "Is there any way to exist without a weapon?" "Yeah," one of the students said. "Stay in the house."

Law enforcement agencies are struggling to keep up with the proliferation of guns. Arrests of kids under 18 for weapons violations jumped by a third from 1976 to 1989. Arrests of teenagers for murder have doubled, while those for rape and robbery have not. "It's not like kids are going out and attacking more people like you and me," says one police official. "They are shooting each other." The inevitable result: 75 percent of juveniles killed by other juveniles are

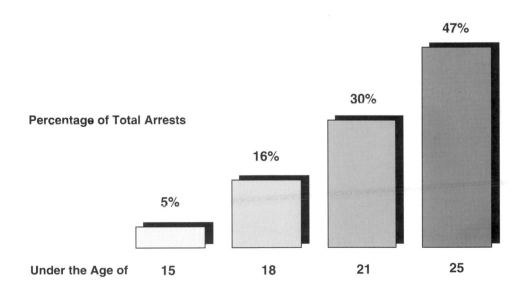

YOUTH AND CRIME

Percentage of Total Arrests

47%

30%

16%

5%

Under the Age of   15   18   21   25

Number of total arrests nationwide in 1990: 14 Million

Source: The U.S. Federal Bureau of Investigation Crime Reports: 1990.

shot to death. In an effort to protect students from becoming gunshot victims, many schools, including more than 50 in New York City, have installed metal detectors and security systems. These metal detectors are designed to detect heavy metal objects like guns or knives. Other schools have hired security guards, effectively giving a prison-like atmosphere to what are supposed to be places of learning.

There are efforts to educate would-be gunslingers as well. In Boston, for example, every public school student caught with a gun is sent to the Barron Assessment & Counseling Center for a five- to ten-day stay. In addition to regular academic work, kids enrolled are provided with intensive counseling, given psychological and educational tests, and work with the center on a plan to improve their lives once they return to school. Especially effective are the visits to local jails where students learn firsthand about the lives of violent inmates. In its ten-year existence, the service has treated more than 1,000 students. Only about five percent of those enrolled become involved with illegal firearms later on.

A similar program in Florida run by the Center to Prevent Handgun Violence and the Dade County Public Schools exposes gun offenders to role-playing therapy, as well as to books and videos intended to deter would-be gunslingers.

TEACHING EMOTIONAL LITERACY

Much violent behavior stems from a general failure to communicate. It comes about because people tend to "react" rather than talk about problems in a careful and productive manner. Many Americans, young and old, do not know how to communicate their angry feelings without attacking others. In response, many schools have begun to experiment with "emotional literacy" programs aimed at teaching young people how to deal with feelings of anger in nonviolent ways.

Under the direction of Shelly Kessler of the Crossroads School in Santa Monica, California, young people enroll in two-hour classes taught by trained therapists. To participate in these voluntary classes, students must agree to confidentiality—promising not to reveal to outsiders what is said during class. Although those enrolled are encouraged not to swear or use profanity, they are not censored and are allowed to say anything they want. The specific intention of this and other programs is to create an atmosphere where anger can be expressed without fear of harmful consequences.

William Kreidler and Dr. Deborah Prothrow-Stith have developed a different program for teaching young people how to prevent violence. Their ten-session course is used in all Boston high schools and at many other schools around the country. The intent of this program is to take the glamour out of violence, to help young people understand its consequences, and to train them in other ways to deal with anger.

According to one public school teacher with more than 15 years experience, "Today's kids are asked to deal with a great deal of frustration. Many come from broken homes, or live with stepparents or with violent uncles or brothers. The poor are routinely exposed and subjected to violence. Kids who are batted around by angry men every time they get out of line have no idea that a dispute might be settled verbally. Either they go along with what's happening or they go home for a gun or a knife. Talking things out is something most of them have never seen happen."

ASSERTIVENESS

In another effort to reduce school violence, some schools have begun to teach communication skills such as assertiveness. Being assertive is a way of letting others know where you stand on an issue that is important to you. Dealing with your feelings and opinions honestly without making yourself right and the other person wrong is a valuable skill you can use all your life. Assertiveness is simply an honest, noncombative response to a situation. For example, "I don't do drugs" is an assertive statement. It does not include a judgment or a putdown of the person who is offering them to you. In contrast, a statement such as "people who use drugs are scum" is like asking for a fight.

Assertiveness means having an attitude that shows dignity and self-respect for yourself and others. Consider the following dialogue between Cary and John:

"I'm not going to go to the all-night block party on Saturday because I've decided to stay home and work on my history report that's due next week."

"That's a stupid report. It won't make a difference to your grade if it's late."

"You may be right, but I want to get it done so I can go water skiing the following weekend."

THE ASSERTIVE ALTERNATIVE

Rhoda McFarland, a teacher who has worked with students making the transition from drug and alcohol abuse programs into public schools has outlined a three-step program in teaching assertiveness:

1. Own the problem and ask for help. This involves open discussion by stating a particular problem. For example, "I have a problem with your raiding my locker and eating my sandwiches."

2. Offer alternatives. Offer another person a chance to help you take action to be rid of the problem. "Maybe you could get out of bed five minutes earlier and make yourself an extra sandwich before you leave for school."

3. Be willing to negotiate. This demonstrates that you're not seeking to put down or insult the other person. "If there isn't enough bread or if you get up late, just let me know. Sometimes I don't eat my apple and you could maybe eat that instead."

"The block party will be a blast—just like last year's."

"You go and have a great time. I'm putting off my fun until next weekend."

In telling John he wasn't going to the block party, Cary did not suggest that John was wrong for wanting to go to the party, or wrong for neglecting a homework assignment. Because Cary avoided making John feel stupid or wrong, John was able to accept Cary's decision without taking offense.

MEDIATION

Many schools plagued by violence are beginning to introduce a new method of resolving conflict called student mediation. More than 300 schools around the country are teaching students how to mediate, or work with people who need a third party to help resolve their problems. Teens on Target in Oakland, California, teaches students how to deal with potentially explosive situations, and sends them out to the schoolyards where they offer their services to students who might otherwise turn to violence.

In San Francisco's "Conflict Manager" program, students are chosen by peers and teachers to receive 16 hours of training in communication and mediation skills. Working as teams, these students learn to listen and assume roles. But they do not police students. It is up to the students with conflicts to approach them and ask for help. Conflict mediators encourage those with problems to sit down formally with two or more mediators and talk things out.

Mediation—at home or in school—is the process of helping two or more persons discuss their grievances honestly but without violence.

Mediators typically volunteer to help with conflicts provided the parties agree to forego name-calling and interrupting. They must also phrase questions to the other party in a nonthreatening, nonjudgmental way. Mediators then listen to both sides of the dispute with an eye to resolving it as simply as possible. Sometimes those involved in a dispute sign a pledge to live in peace. Other disputes are resolved with a handshake. Mediation does not try to persuade the students in conflict to like each other; it simply guides them so they can talk their differences through and make a change.

When it comes right down to it, violence itself is a form of communication. It's a way of saying, "I dislike you enough to hurt you right now." As an alternative to violence, mediation proposes that since violence almost always has unpleasant consequences for the parties involved, it can be or ought to be put on hold until alternatives can be found.

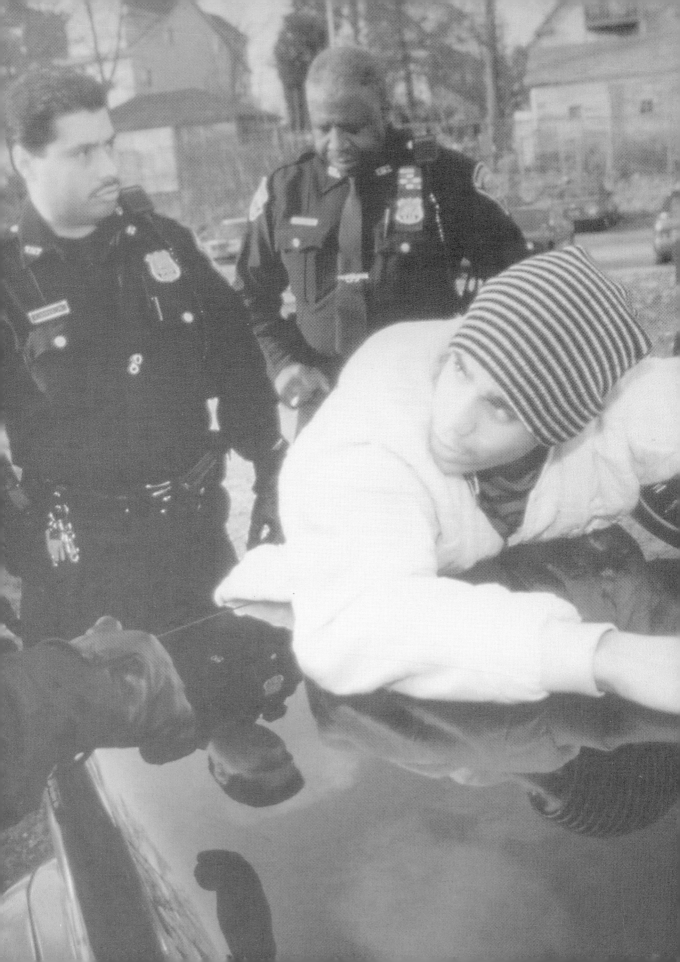

4

LIFE ON THE MEAN STREETS

You got to watch your back all the time. There's never no time to rest. But you adapt to it or you die. That's the law of the street.
—Marcus, age 19

"I couldn't believe I was doing this," remembers Virgil. He was driving a car, a car full of gang members about to shoot someone. "I was scared. I was scared to do anything. I was scared to do nothing. So I just drove."

How did Virgil wind up being involved in a drive-by shooting? How does anyone become caught up in attempted murder? If someone is bored or dissatisfied with the circumstances of his or her life, they are probably hoping for a change or excitement. Bored and lonely, Virgil assumed that any change would be better than what he had. He found out he was wrong.

Virgil had moved to Los Angeles to be with his dad. He wanted to get away from the boring small town where he lived with his mother. His dad had married a woman with a son nearly his own age named Luis. But life in Los Angeles didn't turn out like Virgil had hoped.

Virgil's dad was either working or out all night partying. The first night Virgil was left alone with his stepbrother, Luis lit a joint and offered it to Virgil. He had tried marijuana before and didn't care for it, but Virgil smoked it anyway. When Luis later

The gang lifestyle is spreading to every major city and town in the United States, increasing drug-related crime, graffiti, and drive-by shootings.

introduced Virgil to some of his friends, it became apparent that Luis's gang-style clothing wasn't just a fashion statement. Luis was "down" with a set of Crips, a Los Angeles street gang, and was dealing pot and crack on the streets.

"I started helping Luis deal drugs," said Virgil. "I know it was stupid, but Luis was always so macho when the Crips were around, and I felt I better do what he did."

"One Saturday night we went to a friend's house for a party. Everybody except Luis was 'strapped'— meaning they had guns. I wanted to leave, but if I did I'd embarrass Luis. I couldn't do that."

Embarrassment turned to fear when Virgil discovered that the action that night was going to turn violent. The Crips wanted to "buzz a Bloods party" a few blocks away. One of the Crips told Virgil to drive. "I told them I didn't have a license," remembers Virgil, "and everybody laughed. They thought I was making a joke. Nobody had a license."

Virgil was told to drive very slowly until the Crips' car got close to a crowd of people drinking beer and laughing on the front lawn of a house. When Virgil hit the gas, Luis and the Crips opened fire.

"Everybody was ducking and running," says Luis. "It sounded like a war had broken out. People were screaming and I could hear glass breaking. I don't know if they fired at us. I was shaking."

The next morning Virgil saw a newspaper story about the shooting. Although no one was killed, one gang member had been grazed by a bullet, and an old woman living in the house had been injured in one eye by flying glass. When Virgil saw the photograph of the injured woman with blood streaming down her face, he was reminded of his grandmother.

"That night I decided to go back and live with my mother."

Virgil is pretty sure that Luis won't tell the other gang members where he is, and he knows he'll never say anything to anybody—especially his mom—about what happened the night he went on a drive-by shooting. When he's not grappling with guilt over the shooting, Virgil worries. Sometimes he remembers how exciting life could be in L.A. and how good it felt to be admired by the Crips. He misses having money in his pockets from selling drugs. But whenever he hears about more gang shootings, he worries that his stepbrother Luis is going to die.

CREATING A NEW LIFE

Most people desire change in their lives once in awhile. Some changes are definitely for the better, but change usually involves trade-offs, and sometimes a trade-off may only change one undesirable situation for another. Virgil, for example, felt lonely and lacking in friends; but in L.A. he felt anxious and endangered by peer pressure. He didn't get that much closer to his father, and he discovered that he also missed his mother. Nobody can predict the future with certainty, but it's possible to think proposed changes through, trying to make better decisions.

Virgil got in over his head. He realized he wasn't going to get much attention from his father, and he didn't know about his stepbrother's attitudes and gang connections. It's easy to understand why Virgil wanted to be close to Luis and didn't want to make himself an enemy of the Crips. But Virgil knows now that he could have and should have avoided gang life.

"Sometimes I wish I could go back to L.A. and undo what I did," says Virgil. Like many who have committed crimes or injured others, he has found a way to change direction and do something positive. On Thursday and Saturday afternoons, Virgil helps out in a local church kitchen and then helps deliver hot meals to people who are unable to leave their homes. Doing this has raised his self-esteem and made him feel better about himself. He's also doing better in school, too, and has made new friends.

"He won't say much about it," says Virgil's mother, "but in some ways I think the trip to L.A. was good for him. He used to complain of being bored. But the other night he came back from the library with some books about how to apply to medical school."

GANGS

Juvenile gang life is really nothing new in the United States. However, the violence committed by the juvenile street gangs of yesteryear pales by comparison with the deeds of gangs today.

Like grandfather, like father, like son; in some American communities gang membership has become a family tradition. In Southern California, for instance, police say it is now possible to talk with three, even four generations of gang members. The death toll caused by these circumstances is alarming: In 1988 alone, there were 462 gang-related murders in Los Angeles, fully 107 of them in the small gang-infested community of South Central Los Angeles.

Los Angeles is no longer alone with its gang troubles. A recent study conducted by the University of Southern California reports that 85 percent of all U.S. cities with populations over 100,000 now have significant street gang problems. The *New York Times* recently reported that even a community like Garden City, Kansas, with a population of about 24,000, now has seven gangs. Of the approximately 3,100 known gang members in that state, most are between the ages of 11 and 21.

"Street gang violence is simply individual juvenile violence with a group dynamic," says one gang counselor. "When young people who are not doing well at home or in school, turn away from their families and hit the streets in search of emotional support, conditions are ripe for gang activity....Rap music, television, and movies tend to glorify gang life. A group of kids in Anywhere USA can learn to act like gang members by listening to music, watching television, and buying the right clothes."

Law enforcement experts tend to agree. "One of the troubling things I've seen is how quickly a group of kids can become a gang," an assistant district attorney in Southern California says. "It may start with tagging or just with hanging around, or an interest in a type of music. Pretty soon, they're carrying weapons of one kind or another, and someone gets hurt." But it would be a mistake to think that all young people who hang out together and engage in criminal activities are gang members. Authorities generally reserve the word "gang" to describe groups that take a name for themselves, create an image and codes of loyalty that bind them together against the rest of the world, and violently compete with other gangs over turf or territory—often for drug-money profits.

The price paid by a rival gang member for trespassing on another gang's "turf" can be a beating, a shooting, or even death. In smaller communities, gangs may keep a somewhat lower profile. But many if not most gangs remain sources of trouble. They deal in violence, drugs, and, potentially, death.

Today's gang members have become more sophisticated, more destructive, and less visible. Until recently gang members tended to flaunt their membership. These days, however, many sets and gangs avoid publically identifying themselves as gang members. Some sets of Crips and Bloods, for example, no longer deliberately "fly gang colors" (blue for Crips, red for Bloods). Moreover, where gang members who once dealt drugs also used them and so were more vulnerable to arrest, many of today's gang members have altogether ceased using the drugs they peddle to others. Profits from drug-selling are less likely to be burned up in drug-use by gang members and spent on expensive cars, automatic weapons, portable phones, beepers, music systems, pricey athletic shoes, and other fashionable sportswear instead. These high-status trappings have provided gangs with the ability to leave one community for another. They have also proved useful in the recruitment of new members.

The fact that a few young people in a poor neighborhood can afford to buy and enjoy such status items while others cannot makes gang life look very appealing to inner city youths whose lives have been marked by want. Young kids willing to run errands for successful gangs and drug dealers are often given gifts, cash, and recruited to full-scale membership.

In many cases, say experts, the most dangerous individuals are not so much established gang members as "wannabes," those seeking to be recruited by a gang or set. Younger males and females looking to impress established members with their courage have committed extraordinarily violent acts in the hope of becoming full-fledged gang members. Peer pressure, physical protection, and financial gain are some of the reasons for joining gangs. Belonging to a group with their own traditions and rituals is also influential. Gangs often adhere to rigid styles of dress, wearing only particular brands and kinds of clothing. Many new members are required to adopt nicknames, obtain tattoos, learn hand signals to communicate with fellow gang members, and to mark "turf" with graffiti.

Because gang members are frequently arrested, injured, or killed, violent street gangs must continue to recruit new members. Tragically, while some people are eager to become gang members, others join up only to be free from intimidation and harassment by gang members. For some, gang membership is simply a form of survival.

What can you do to avoid being recruited or victimized by street gangs? How can you avoid street gang violence? For one thing, you can make it a point to learn about gangs in the area where you live. If gangs in your area fly gang colors, learn what they are and avoid dressing in those colors. Hundreds of people have been beaten, robbed, and killed for wearing the wrong color at the wrong time and place. Learn about any other rites or practices of a local gang and avoid seeming either to imitate or ridicule them.

Discuss your predicament with your parents, teachers, counselors, and trusted friends who may be able to help you keep from coming to the attention of gangs. If gangs are particularly popular in your neighborhood, talk to your parents about your hopes and fears and investigate the possibility of attending school in other neighborhoods less haunted by gang violence.

TOUGH PLAYGROUNDS

C arson had just bought a great basketball. He phoned his buddy Jesse and they agreed to spend a couple of hours shooting baskets at a school playground near Jesse's apartment. Jesse reminded Carson that he should be cautious in Jesse's neighborhood because some mean kids roamed the streets, and muggings were common. Before going out, Carson snapped on a heavy gold chain around his neck that his brother Tom hardly ever wore. It looked good with his Chicago Bulls tee shirt.

"I went to the playground early to practice my jump shot," says Carson. Unfortunately, his new basketball attracted attention. A couple of taller guys came over and asked if they could shoot a few hoops. After a few minutes, a muscular teen on a small bike wheeled into the yard and gestured for the ball. Carson thought he wanted to take a couple of shots while riding the bike. Instead, the kid tucked the ball under his arm.

"I want my ball back," Carson said. It was all he could think of to say. The boy on the bike had a folding knife in his hand.

Some teens become the victims of violence by venturing into a neighborhood where gang members protect their "turf."

"All right," the thief grinned. "You can have the ball back. But you have to pay me twenty-five dollars."

"Twenty-five dollars!"

"Five dollars because you ruined the net I hung there last week, and twenty dollars rent on the playground. Give me twenty-five and I'll give it back."

"I don't have any money," Carson said. He looked at the other guys standing around. They did not seem exactly hostile, yet there was something about the way they stood there, as if warning him not to press the matter. Carson decided to walk away.

"When do you want to pay me the money?" the thief demanded.

Now Carson felt he was really in danger. "Next Saturday," he said.

"That's agreeable to me," the thief said. "Same time next Saturday. Just come around here and ask for Monkey Bike."

Dejected and feeling like a coward, Carson decided to get a bus home. He chose to take a shortcut to another bus stop that would take him closer to home. But he walked right into harm's way. The next thing he knew a man put a pistol to Carson's head.

"I thought of my family and started to pray," said Carson. "The man ripped the gold chain off my neck. Then he jumped inside a car that pulled up and he was gone."

Carson started to run. His legs felt rubbery, but he ran as fast as he could. Several blocks away, he found a cop. Carson had never been so glad to see anyone in his life. The cop was interested, but seemed in no hurry to catch the thieves. He took Carson's name, address, and phone number, and advised him not to come into the neighborhood by himself anymore.

Apart from taking his brother's gold chain without asking permission, what had Carson done wrong? The answer is, nothing. He just didn't use common sense.

BLAMING THE VICTIM

"Blaming the victim" means holding the victim responsible for a serious crime instead of the criminal. That night Carson's father said to him, "I told you before to stay out of that neighborhood. You get no sympathy from me at all."

Although Carson's decision to go alone into a bad neighborhood might not have been too smart, he didn't deserve to be robbed. We all make bad decisions at times. The boy who took Carson's basketball and the man who stole his brother's gold chain are guilty of much more than failing to use good judgment. But often people don't speak out against such crimes. Why?

According to psychologists, blaming the victim is a common occurrence. Sometimes it is easier to blame the victim than to solve the crime, or to address the problems underlying the crime. But blaming the victim is destructive. The people doing the blaming use it as an excuse to avoid taking action. In the case of Carson, as long as his father and the police believe Carson was responsible for what happened, they are unlikely to seek out or discipline Monkey Bike or the other thief.

You can help lessen juvenile violence by not blaming the victim. Focus on the perpetrator, the criminal. Do what you can to increase your own personal safety and that of your friends.

- *Know where you're going before you leave the house.* If Carson had asked Jesse a few more questions about the neighborhood, he might have decided to play with Jesse on a different court. Most cities have "bad" neighborhoods. Avoid placing yourself at risk.
- *Don't travel alone.* Going alone into an unknown area is more dangerous than traveling with a friend or two who know the territory. However, ranging into a "bad" neighborhood with a group of friends can also invite trouble—you might be inviting yourself to a gang fight.
- *Don't flaunt desirable property.* Carson could have taken an older, less desirable ball. By topping off his wardrobe with a gold chain, Carson invited trouble.

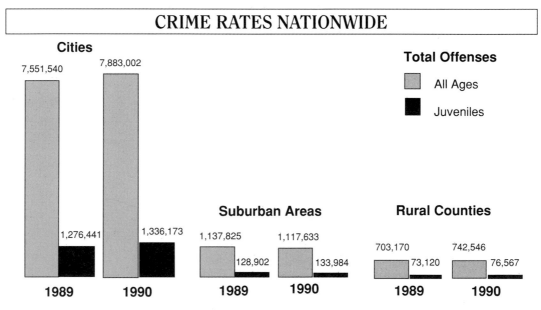

The number of juveniles charged with crimes—ranging from burglary and mugging to rape and murder—has increased nationwide. Whether you live in a large city or a small farming community, the percentage of juveniles who commit crimes remains fairly constant. Knowing that crime can occur anywhere gives you an important defense: awareness. Paying attention to your surroundings will help lessen your chances of becoming a target.

Source: FBI Uniform Crime Reports

Some people might think Carson should have fought back. Was Carson a coward? It's true that Carson felt afraid, but he was not paralyzed by his fears. He stood his ground at first, looking to reclaim his ball and trying to communicate with Monkey Bike. It was only when he noticed the anxiety of the others that Carson began to believe that Monkey Bike was dangerous and decided to retreat.

How about the gold chain mugging? Had Carson so much as flinched, he might have been shot before the mugger even had decided whether to shoot him. Triggers and bullets are faster than many decisions. Many guns have gone off before the shooter decided to shoot.

Carson's older brother Tom talked about what he thought was really important: "If you were found dead in a strange neighborhood and if no witnesses ever appeared to say what happened, how would I ever know if you had been brave or not? I'm sure I would have felt very bad that you were dead. But you know, in a way, with a little bit of my mind, I might think you had been stupid for going into that neighborhood alone and for not giving up a lousy basketball in order to live the rest of your life."

Carson made three good decisions on the day he lost his basketball and gold chain. First, he backed away from Monkey Bike's knife. Second, he didn't resist the man with the gun. Third, he reported the crimes to the police and provided descriptions of the thieves. Carson did something about the problem of juvenile violence—for himself and for others. Report crimes as quickly as possible after they've happened. Even if there are no arrests at first, police will notice patterns of crime in specific areas and change their patrols to try and catch more criminals in high-crime areas.

USING PUBLIC TRANSPORTATION

L isa and Heather were practicing for a high school play. Knowing they could get a bus home by using their bus passes, they spent the last of their money on pizza before going home. It was dark when they walked to the bus stop.

Soon after they boarded the bus, three older boys got on and sat right behind them. They were drunk and tried to start a conversation. Lisa and Heather pretended not to hear them. When the boys started talking dirty, the girls tried to drown out the vulgar language by reciting their lines to each other.

When Lisa got off, things became more unpleasant for Heather. One of the boys leaned over and told her she had a beautiful body. Heather was too scared to say anything. When her stop came, she got off quickly. The boys followed.

"I ran," recalls Heather. "I could hear them running after me. Luckily, I had a head start. I ran into a supermarket two blocks from my house. The manager of the store was very understanding and offered to drive me home." At that point, Heather didn't trust anybody. She asked if she could use the phone. Her father came to pick her up.

Heather and Lisa should be free to come and go as they please. Although they weren't physically injured, they were frightened in a way they are likely to remember all their lives. They didn't do anything wrong, but they could have done some things differently.

- *Always carry emergency money for a phone call.* Put a few quarters aside and don't use them for spending money. Arrange for a ride home after dark. Avoid the bus or subway late at night.
- *Whenever possible, seek visibility.* If a bus is mostly empty, sit toward the front. A bus driver can't come to your aid if he or she can't see you. Don't be afraid to tell the driver if someone is bothering you.
- *Get up and move if necessary.* If someone is talking to you, or if you don't like the way they're looking at you, move to another seat.
- *Stay together when there's trouble.* Parting company as the girls did was not a good decision because Heather was left alone.
- *Avoid appearing like an easy victim.* If she'd had some training in assertiveness, Heather might have said something to convince the three bullies that she was not and would not be an easy victim. Heather might have said, "I'm sorry you feel you have to talk to me that way. I'm not a threat to you, but I will tell the driver to use his radio to call for help if you keep talking to me."
- *Seek a safe haven.* Heather showed good sense in seeking the safety of the supermarket. Even though the supermarket manager's offer of a ride home was probably a sincere one, Heather's decision to call her father was the wisest.

Although you may be comfortable riding the bus and traveling alone in your own neighborhood, be sure to travel with friends whenever you go to an unfamiliar area.

AVOID MISUNDERSTANDINGS

Simon, Lee, and Becky left home early one evening for a concert to be held at a downtown arena. A group of kids who were drinking beer and smoking pot got into line behind them and started joking around. They offered to share their joints with Simon and Lee, who politely said no. One of the group asked Lee to hold his beer while he went to talk to a friend. No sooner did Lee take the bottle than a security guard demanded he get rid of it.

Lee said the bottle didn't belong to him, that he was holding it for someone else. The guard said that unless he poured the beer out immediately, he and his friends would not be admitted to the concert.

Becky got angry and called the security guard a name. The guard called for back-up and told Becky, "That's enough." Neither she nor Lee would be admitted to the concert. Simon stepped toward the guard to protest, and the guard grabbed him by the arm. That's when the fight started. Two of the teens from the beer-drinking group got involved, kicking and punching.

"When it was all over," said Lee, "all of us were handcuffed, driven away, and locked up."

Eventually, their parents came to pick them up. Simon had a broken nose and an injured finger. Lee had bruises from being hit with a nightstick. Becky had a swollen lip. To their surprise, they were charged with being minors in possession of alcohol, being drunk and disorderly, violating a law against drinking on the streets, creating a public disturbance, assaulting a police officer, and criminal possession of marijuana. In fact, they had not been drinking, had not been drunk, had acted in self-defense, and were only guilty of coming to one another's aid. None of them had even tried the marijuana.

The next few weeks involved several meetings with attorneys. The police agreed to drop all the charges in exchange for an agreement that Lee and his friends would not file brutality charges against the police or sue the security guard company.

The three friends, the security guards, and the police became caught up in the sort of misunderstanding that is all too

CHALLENGING AUTHORITY

When police or security officials are involved in a confrontation, clear, polite communication is what is required—the sooner and the clearer the better. A reluctance to cooperate or do what you're told is usually interpreted as belligerence.

Police officers can't read people's minds and don't have the time to determine their intentions. Their job is to prevent people from breaking the law and arrest them when they are making trouble.

Because young people are often inclined to commit crimes that put both themselves and the police at risk, police sometimes act first and ask questions later. Failing to follow orders from a police officer will surely result in legal problems.

Avoiding trouble in public can mean making simple adjustments in your behavior, from not loitering or drinking in public to respecting authority.

common in crowded public places. Because of earlier experiences, police and security teams are often nervous before rock and rap concerts. The security guard was instructed to keep alcohol and drinkers out of the arena. He naturally assumed that Lee, who was holding the bottle, was drinking. When Becky got angry and offensive, the security guard decided to bar both of them from the concert. Simon's stepping toward the guard was interpreted as threatening. The police came to break up a fight. Later the police found marijuana on two of the other kids and wrongly charged all five with possession of drugs.

How could this have been handled differently? When confronted by the security guard, Lee could have simply poured out the beer and asked him to remain there to explain why he had to get rid of it. Becky should have stayed out of it. Name-calling doesn't help.

Simon's father made a good point. "Drugs are illegal, and since you're under 21, so is alcohol. I hope if you learn anything from this it will be to never hold, deliver, handle, or stand guard over somebody else's illegal property— friend or no friend."

5

VIOLENCE, RACE, AND BIAS

*Racism? Yeah, I know what it is. Even my counselor said he
was surprised that I got a "D" in math—since I was
"Chinese."*
—David, age 17

David, a 17-year-old Korean-American, was jumped and beaten by three white guys on the street. "It was about the worst thing that ever happened to me," David recalls. "I was all alone and felt like I was fighting for my life. One of them would move on me and I'd turn to defend myself and boom, I'd be hit by one of the others. My clothes got ripped and I was staggering around just trying to stay up on my feet. That was when one of them called me a Chinese wimp. 'Three of your kind robbed my cousin,' one of them said. They had stopped hitting me then, so I stepped back and said, 'I don't know what you're talking about. Anyway, I'm Korean.' That's when one of them laughed and said, 'What's the difference? You Koreans are bleeping Chinamen anyway.' That got me mad. As beaten up as I was, if I'd had the strength I would have hit him just for saying that. Not that I'm prejudiced against the Chinese. It's just the ignorance, the arrogance of not knowing that the Chinese and Koreans are separate people really bothered me."

Alec and Tom, both 15, were beaten by several African-Americans who had just heard about a black man who had been set on fire by some white men in

*Racism is one of the most difficult problems facing our society.
It continues to be a cause of violence between juveniles as well
as adults, even infecting our schools.*

Florida. "I remember them hitting me and saying something about setting people on fire and stuff," Alec remembers. "I came home and cleaned up. When my dad came home I told him what had happened and that I hadn't asked for trouble, that these guys just jumped me, talking about burning black people. Dad said that maybe they were talking about three white guys in Florida who had set a black man on fire. I'd never burn or attack anybody. And I've never even been to Florida."

Lenny, 16, was chased by a racially mixed group of kids because one of their sisters had said that she'd been slapped by an Italian guy. One of the attackers knew Lenny's ancestry was Italian, and that was good enough.

Racist outbursts or attacks can be directed against anyone at any time. Often they are somebody's idea of revenge for an earlier incident—often, an incident totally unrelated to the victim. The alleged incident may not have been real, just imagined.

No one is born knowing what race he or she belongs to. In fact, we know nothing of racial identity or pride until we are taught. When somebody is taught to treat people according to how they look or speak or what they believe, that is called "prejudice," or "prejudging" someone. Often an innocent person is insulted or injured simply because of prejudice or something racial that supposedly happened in the past. Like other forms of violence, racism is cyclical. Violence does not end violence, and racial violence does not end racial violence; it merely provides somebody with an excuse to act out yet another racist episode, and so on. In this way the wheel of racism grinds us all down, robbing us of our dignity as human beings, and reducing us to ethnic groups at war.

INTERRACIAL TENSION

J oanne gets straight A's, sings in the glee club, and is a popular cheerleader at her high school. Her friend Jamal is a whiz at math, sings in a hiphop group, and was written up in the newspaper as one of the best high school baseball pitchers in the city.

Jamal is African-American, and Joanne is white. Although they would like to date each other, so far they have only met and talked secretly. Joanne has a brother named Archer who belongs to a skinhead motorcycle gang. Like many skinheads, Archer believes in the superiority of the white race. To hear Archer tell it, life would be perfect if it weren't for African-Americans and Jews.

One day Archer saw Joanne talking with Jamal. He confronted her later and slapped her face and threatened to kill Jamal if she continued to see him. When Joanne told their mother about the incident, she sided with Joanne. Archer found out and slapped his mother, too.

"Skinhead" and so-called "Neo-Nazi" gangs of white youths in America are a concern to people who believe those groups promote racism.

"Archer had been out of control for a while before that happened," Joanne admits. "He'd bullied me and smacked me around since we were small. But when he slapped my mom, something in me snapped. For me, that was the beginning of the end.

"Later I started thinking about it and realized I had a conflict about Jamal. He knew that my brother was a skinhead and that he called himself a neo-Nazi, but I didn't think I should tell Jamal that Archer had slapped me and my mom. I mean, I was worried that Jamal might get mad and go after my brother. Jamal can handle himself, but to tell the truth, I didn't want to see either Jamal or Archer hurt. And I was worried that Archer might get his whole gang out after Jamal. The last thing Jamal and I needed, I thought, was to start some local race war between skinheads and the minorities they hate so much."

Although he didn't know about the slapping incidents, Jamal had some concerns of his own about dating Joanne.

"My dad was an activist in the sixties," he says. "Just before I was born, he became a Muslim. Generally, he believes that the Islamic religion is about the only religion that has ever been fair to people of color. Though I'm not strongly religious myself, I do love and respect my family. My mom is a little less hard core than my dad, but even she thinks people should stick to their own kind and color."

Jamal and Joanne believe that people—black or white or any other color—should be left alone to develop friendships and relationships with one another. However, Jamal understands that in the real world, dating Joanne would put both of them at risk. Joanne doesn't want to become a source of trouble between Jamal and his father. They have been thinking about whether to date each other for several months, but unfortunately there isn't always an easy answer to a problem involving racial violence.

"My mom has always been real big on keeping problems in the immediate family," Joanne says. "But after Archer slapped her, I thought, 'No, I'm not keeping quiet this time.' That night after my mom was in bed I called my uncle Perry, a lawyer who lives in Oklahoma. He said, 'Look, you've got two problems, not one. Your first problem has to do with Archer, and your second problem has to do with Jamal. But we've got to deal with first things first. Archer is obviously a danger to you and your mother.'"

After getting Joanne's permission, Perry called Joanne's mother and told her about his conversation with Joanne. He said that it was clear that Archer had never learned to deal with his anger, and that his anger posed a threat to everybody around him.

"I told her the only way Archer would get the help he needed was to admit he had problems and seek help for them," says Perry. "I called an attorney living near Joanne and eventually persuaded Joanne and her mother to apply for a restraining order against Archer. The restraining order required Archer to get out of the house and prevented him from trying to contact either Joanne or her mother." It meant that Archer could be arrested for even coming to the house, but it didn't entirely solve the problem. It certainly didn't change Archer's mind about race relations.

TOUGH LOVE

On Perry's recommendation, Joanne and her mother attended family therapy sessions to help them understand their complicated feelings regarding Archer. The therapist introduced them to the principles of "tough love."

The philosophy of tough love acknowledges the power that love holds over family members. It recognizes that we cannot stop and start loving our families with the flip of a switch. It also understands that each human being has the right to make his or her own important personal decisions without being beaten or threatened by family members. Although it recognizes that drug, alcohol, and people abusers exploit human kindness to further their own self-destruction, tough love is not cold or indifferent. It states that a person has the right to ruin his or her own life if that is what he or she chooses to do. Those who employ the concept of tough love learn that the only thing they can do when another person behaves in a self-destructive manner is to look out for themselves first, and cease doing anything that encourages the other person to continue to behave self-destructively.

"Archer was mad when he found out we kicked him out of the house," Joanne admits. "He said we were hopeless cases and weren't worth trying to help. When he said that, I felt both sad and relieved. I figured that whether or not he seeks help, at least he'd leave us alone for a while. But it also gave me another thought. At that point I told Jamal about Archer and the slapping business, as well as the restraining order. It seemed important to let Jamal know that he should watch his back. In fact, I should have told him sooner than I did."

"I went through a lot of emotions when Joanne told me about what Archer did," Jamal stated. "And when she told me about his threats against me, at first I was mad at her, thinking she had put me in danger in order to protect her brother. Once we talked that through—and I'm glad we did—I had to go away and think. I thought, I don't want trouble, but as far as I'm concerned, if I feel like I have to be looking over my shoulder, then I've already got trouble."

Jamal remembered some stories that his father had told him about his great grandfather's experience with the Ku Klux Klan. "My dad had told me one thing that I should know about racists is that they are bad when they are in a big group of people. He said, 'You don't hear about any black people that were hanged by a single Klansman.' Racists who might act badly in a group are often as sweet as little sheep dogs when they're alone. His idea was that these people are so scared of the people they hate because they make them into monsters instead of human beings. So I figured I could apply that to Archer.

"I saw him downtown about a week later, first time I think I ever saw him without a big can of beer in his hand. He looked clean and sober, so I walked over to him, told him my name, that I knew that he hated black people, that I was a friend of Joanne's, and that if he wanted to talk about anything I'd like to get done with the talking right then and there so I could get on with my life. The dude started saying something about my honesty and tried to tell me I was a credit to my race. I said, 'I ain't a credit to anything. I'm just telling you that if you want to talk to me about me or my friends, now's a good time.' He shrugged his shoulders and said not to worry, that he didn't have a sister. When he said he didn't have a sister, I pitied him and figured that I wasn't going to have a problem with him."

Joanne and Jamal met for coffee soon afterward. They both felt happy that Archer seemed ready to leave them alone. They still would like to date, but they realize that while extremists like Archer are fairly rare, troublemakers are more common. There's still the resistance of Jamal's parents. Nothing is settled, but if Jamal draws on his directness and patience, he may be able to win them over in time.

RESISTING RACISM

Even if two people like Joanne and Jamal are successful in dealing with racial problems that arise from within their own families, they will still be faced with what every interracial couple has always had to contend with: A range of social responses that range from disappointment to downright hostility.

Chances are good that if you are a teenager living in a multiracial community, you have already become familiar with the ugly face of racism. What can you do about it? On a large scale, maybe little or nothing. On a personal level, you can almost certainly do a great deal.

Beware of referring to people in terms of their race. Most racist names or epithets only further inflame racism—even when they are used jokingly or by members of that race. Second, take the positive approach. Instead of applying labels to people you don't know, become informed and look past the obvious.

Respect others. Don't insist that other people be bound by your beliefs or experiences. This calls for empathy. Remember that in many places on earth, you would be a racial or ethnic minority and subject to prejudice. Acknowledge that no one has the right to limit an individual's freedom because of his or her race or beliefs. Be willing to grant friends and strangers the right to form their own friendships.

Don't stereotype. People are endowed with a humanity that is more significant than their racial origins. Every stereotype is an oversimplified and generally inaccurate observation that labels someone as one thing and one thing only—fat, short, bald, brown, Jewish, elderly, vegetarian. None of these qualities can define a human being. They are merely attributes—physical, cultural, or conscious choices that do not define a person.

Learn a little history. Very few groups in the United States escaped persecution for race or ethnic origins. In the early years of the United States, the Irish, Italians, Poles, Hispanics, Germans, Native Americans, Chinese, and Japanese were all persecuted because of their place of birth. Catholics, Jews, and Mormons have all experienced discrimination because of their religion. Yet all of these people have survived and made significant and essential contributions to the American way of life. Discover and believe in the importance of your own background; then seek the meaning and beauty in other cultural traditions. From music to rocketry, America owes much of its influence in the world to men and women who came here from other lands and found a way to belong and participate in American life.

Recognize and expose racial and sexual stereotyping. When you hear others say that white men can't jump, women can't do math, African-Americans are this way, Koreans are that way, say something. Ask them where they got such an idea. With even a little knowledge of world and cultural history, you'll realize that superficial stereotypes do not hold up to informed, intelligent discussion.

Seek out opportunities to share activities with others of different races and backgrounds. Learn a foreign language. Make friends with people who don't dress like you. Expose yourself to music from other cultures. See movies by filmmakers from other countries. Visit museums to find out about other places. Be an example for others who want to break down barriers but are afraid to do so.

Interracial couples still face many difficulties in society because some people cannot accept them.

BIAS FOR ITS OWN SAKE

A lvin and four of his friends went skateboarding outside the local mall. While they were taking a break, a homeless man asked them for a dollar. Alvin said he didn't have a dollar, and Wally said he'd give him a towel and some soap so he could wash up and get a job. When the man muttered something about their expensive skateboards, Richie punched the man twice in the face. Then he kicked him with his foot and told him to get lost. Wally said maybe the homeless man could get a job as a punching bag, and Richie laughed and bounced a soda can off the man's back.

Two days later, when he was on his way to Wally's house, Alvin saw the homeless man again. He noticed that the man had a black eye, probably from being hit by Richie. Alvin gave him 50 cents and asked him about his black eye. The man said that he'd been beaten up but couldn't remember who had hit him. The man rolled up his sleeve and showed Alvin two tattoos. He said he'd gotten them when he was fighting in Vietnam, adding that he had seen many of his friends killed in the war. Then he showed Alvin a recent photograph of himself standing proudly in front of the Vietnam War Memorial in Washington D.C.

"When I got to Wally's house I felt pretty low," Alvin said. "I was thinking of what it would be like to have fought in a war and seen my friends killed. I told Wally what happened, and because his uncle had been killed in the war, he felt even worse than I did. When we called Richie to tell him, he was not impressed. He called homeless people bums and said they all made up stories about having been in Vietnam or about suffering from some disease in order to get people's pity. I tried to tell him about the photograph and the tattoos, but Richie said I was a wimp and that homeless people were just parasites and we ought to round them all up and give them a choice of taking a job or going to jail.

"I decided I really don't need to have a guy like Richie for a friend. He doesn't care about anybody but himself and always has reasons for disliking everybody. Life is too short to hang around people who think only of themselves or think that the country has been ruined by this or that group of people. I can't imagine how somebody could reach Richie. I guess he's just going to keep on abusing people he doesn't like until he gets in serious trouble."

Alvin has hit on one way of avoiding biased behavior. He has decided to make an effort to socialize only with those who are decent people capable of sympathizing with others.

Psychologists believe that those who are about to engage in violent or racist behavior, like Richie, distance themselves from their victims by dehumanizing them. Before hurting another person, an attacker must convince himself that the person about to be attacked is without worth or merit. Richie believed all homeless people are bums. Often abusers tell themselves that the intended victim belongs to a group that is already creating harm. For example: White people are all racists; therefore, it is okay if I hurt a white person. Or, Hispanic people in poor neighborhoods are lazy. Or, gays try to molest young children and want to ruin the American family. These are typical biased or racist reasons offered by those who would persecute others.

HOW RIVALRIES GET OUT OF HAND

The phone rings. "Hello, this is Kimberly's friend Janet. There's been a big fight at the basketball game and somebody fell on Kimberly and hurt her leg. A nurse is putting some ice on it. She's all right but she asked me to call and see if you would come over and pick us up."

Kimberly's dad Jim drives over to Jefferson High School and meets the girls. By the time he gets there many people have left the gym and the situation is calm. Kimberly's leg is bruised and she can hardly walk, but she is not seriously injured.

"We were just sitting there watching the game when behind us we heard these guys starting to fight. We were going to move out of the way when these other guys started fighting and one of them fell on me," Kimberly tells her dad.

"What was the fight about?" Jim asks.

"The kids from Lincoln hate us," Janet says. "They've always hated us."

On the ride home, Jim remembers his own high school days. He, too, had attended Jefferson and he, too, remembered fights with students from Lincoln High—fights in the football stadium, fights at wrestling matches. "Dad," Kimberly asks, "why do the kids from Lincoln hate us? It's not like it's a race thing. Both the schools have the same kind of kids."

Jim has no answer, because he sees that this high school rivalry is unchanged from 20 years ago. Lincoln versus Jefferson. It's a feud based on a grudge that's become a tradition. Not all bias or prejudice has racial or even cultural overtones. In the case of the Lincoln and Jefferson feud, something—maybe some trivial aspect of school "honor"—may have triggered it. It happened so long ago that nobody can remember what it was. But the rivalry lives on in the name of "school spirit." Victims of such "school spirit" can include principals, coaches, teachers, and students who take a normal athletic rivalry and turn it into an unhealthy obsession with the "enemy."

A very similar situation happens with gangs in neighborhoods. Because many gangs are comprised of ethnic groups (Hispanics, Asians, whites, etc.), gang behavior promotes and thrives on racism that often leads to the destruction of its own members.

6

VIOLENCE TOWARD WOMEN AND GIRLS

My boyfriend's cool as long as I don't talk to my girlfriends
too long or laugh at his friend's jokes.
—Tammi, age 15

"At first, I was flattered he seemed to care so much," Joyce said. "Then my boyfriend Eddie began to find faults with little things I did, like the way I carried my books, the way I fixed my hair, why I talked to this person or that person. Then slowly, he started telling me what to do. At first, I did whatever he asked, hoping to please him. But he was never really pleased. He just criticized something else. Pretty soon, to keep from being scolded, I was asking his advice about everything. That's when my friend, Constance, warned me that I was in an abusive relationship. But I thought she was nuts."

Joyce was made leader of a history project that involved five students. This meant she had to consult with other team members. When Eddie saw her talking to Bowen, who was on her team, he stormed off and didn't meet her after classes or drive her home from school as usual. That night Bowen called Joyce to discuss the class project. "Something weird happened when I came out of school this afternoon," he told her. "Somebody had smashed the windshield of my car." Although Bowen didn't connect the incident to Eddie, Joyce was almost certain that Eddie had broken his windshield.

A couple whose relationship is dominated by violent arguments and physical abuse has a serious problem.

The next morning Joyce started walking to school, certain that since Eddie hadn't called or spoken to her, he wouldn't come by her house. About three blocks from school, she heard the roar of a car engine. Eddie came racing up the street and, seeing her, drove his car up the curb and onto somebody's front lawn. He jumped out of the car, grabbed her, and practically threw her in the car. He called her names and accused her of having a crush on Bowen. When she denied it and asked him why he had broken Bowen's windshield, he slapped her. While she cried, he went into a rage about all her "faults."

"Somehow, the moment he started ranting in the car, I stopped crying and knew I was going to have to break up with him," Joyce recalled. "I'd seen this program on TV about abused women. I opened my purse to fix my makeup, and in the mirror it was like I saw one of those women's faces in my own. They talked about how sweet and kind and forgiving their husbands and boyfriends could be. The slap and Eddie's rage really woke me up."

Joyce's friend Constance remembers their conversation. "I was sympathetic and gave her lots of hugs," she says, "but I wasn't really shocked he'd slapped her. My aunt had been in an abusive relationship and I was sure Joyce was in the early stages of one. About three weeks before he slapped her, I had this talk with Joyce and said, 'I never see you anymore because it's like your whole life is a clock that's set to Eddie's schedule. When are you going to wake up? When is your alarm going to go off?'"

OUT OF CONTROL

"It's strange," Joyce admits, "how subtle it all was, his taking over my life like that. It wasn't until I decided to break up with Eddie that I was really scared of him. I went away for a couple of weekends and then made careful plans and broke with him very slowly and gently. After the slap, I didn't think anything about how I was losing Eddie. I told myself, 'I've got to get out of this. I've got to make good plans.' I stopped thinking about him at all, and all I thought about was planning our breakup."

"I went crazy at first," Eddie remembers. "I broke things and did other things I'm not proud of. It was my mother who first got through to me. In all my years living with her, she'd never talked about why she had left my dad. Once she figured out what was going on, she admitted that she'd left him because he was controlling and jealous. Then she bought me a plane ticket to go visit my dad and his family. I got out there and saw that his third wife and her kids are totally scared of him. Secretly, I think they hate him. I came back thinking, 'Wow, my dad is totally alone. He doesn't have a clue about how people feel about him under their fears.' I came back, helped Bowen put in a used windshield, and told him what had happened. We ended up talking about our dads for a long time.

Males who are continually abusive to their girlfriends—either physically or mentally— cannot control their emotions, and should seek counseling.

"It's not like I have my act totally together yet, but now, when I start to have possessive feelings, I back off. I've hurt a couple of girls' feelings in being too distant, maybe, but I don't want to go back to the old Eddie. I used to have too much self-confidence, but it was just made up of not caring about what other people wanted. Now I think about whether I want to kiss my date goodnight. I used to talk about myself all the time or not listen to what girls said. Now I try to ask them questions like, 'How do you feel about this, about that?' I figure, as long as I'm asking questions and listening, I'm not my old self."

Eddie called Joyce for the first time in two months. "Eddie seems to be changing," Joyce said afterward. "He phones me occasionally and always begins by apologizing for the way he was. Actually, that makes me nervous, a little. But then he always adds what I want to hear—that he doesn't want to get back together, but just find out how things are going and tell me what he's thinking about. We end up talking about some kids at school who behave a lot like we used to. Eddie joked that we should start a 'Lighten Up Club.'"

"When I came back from visiting my dad," Eddie said, "I felt suddenly real close to my mom. It was like a part of me in the past had been angry with her for not telling me more about why my dad didn't live with us. We had a long talk about things and she said that she thought maybe her mistake was in not setting more limits for me when I was younger. Maybe she's right."

FROM SLAPPING TO BEATING

Have you ever heard the phrase "rule of thumb?" It originated in the English Middle Ages when the rule of thumb made it acceptable for a man to beat his wife with a stick no thicker than a thumb. In the 1400s, a monk named Cherubino Siena wrote *Rules of Marriage.* In it he advised, "Scold [your wife] sharply, bully and terrify her. If that doesn't work—take up a stick and beat her soundly." Five hundred years old or not, these bits of historical trivia show that violence toward women goes back a long time.

Juveniles in the 1990s who are violent toward women are in the process of becoming abusive adults with more in common with their ancestors than they might like to admit. Experts on domestic abuse and sexual violence say that many abusers have often been abused as children—either sexually, physically, or emotionally.

Many males who mistreat females grew up in households watching their fathers mistreat their mothers. What about the women who take it? As you might guess, many women who are abused grew up in households watching their mothers being abused.

Abusers tend to fall into two categories: "hostile" abusers and "entitled" abusers. Although hostile abusers are widely regarded as the most violent and dangerous of the two, entitled abusers are also dangerous, particularly in close relationships like the one between Eddie and Joyce. Eddie, whose mother admitted that she'd found it difficult to discipline him, felt that he was entitled to do whatever he wanted—until Joyce finally had enough.

In his book, *Violent Men,* Hans Toch says that people like Eddie will normally go on using criticism, threats, intimidation, and violence until they are stopped, punished, and obliged to acknowledge their problem and do something about it. Eddie is highly unusual in that he had an insightful, helpful mother who enabled him to see the unhappy reflection of his father in himself. He's doing something about his problem. If you're a male, what about you?

Do you fall for a girl and then try to change her once you get to know her? Do you dislike her friends? When you go out together, how often do you do what she wants? Do you "keep an eye on her" so that she won't go out with other guys? Are you the "jealous type?" When you're upset with her, do you stop talking to her? Do you pout or sulk or throw temper tantrums? Have you ever called her a bad name? What would you do if she said you should each date other people for a while? Do you have any female friends you don't date? Are you so afraid that she'll break up with you that the thought of it sends you into a panic?

If you answered yes to any of these questions, you may already be in trouble or headed for trouble. There's one sure-fire question you can ask your girlfriend that will let you know where you stand: "Have I ever acted in such a way or done anything to make you feel afraid of me?"

If her answer is yes, then you've taken the first step to making some positive changes in your life. The second step is to listen to what she says without making excuses. Hear her out. Experts estimate that about one male in six eventually abuses his girlfriend or wife. If your girlfriend is willing to be honest with you, you're being given a chance to become a better and happier man.

What can you do about your violent behavior? Think about your excuses for your behavior. Put them into a few words. Chances are they will fall into one of two categories:

1. *I was out of control.* If this is your excuse, realize one thing. Being out of control is not an excuse; it is an admission. What you are admitting is that you lost control of your behavior. It's not uncommon to have feelings that are difficult to control, but the need for self-control is crucial. Those who don't learn to control such feelings end up doing great harm to themselves and others. They often end up in prisons or mental institutions.

2. *She made me do it.* Your girlfriend may have done something that made you angry, but you are not a puppet. Let's say you were jealous and slapped her. There was a moment between when you were tempted to slap her and when you followed through. In that moment you made your decision to be violent. Next time, make a different decision.

Violence has a tendency to escalate over time. In some ways, like substance abuse, violence provides a temporary feeling of power. Like the highs from drugs and alcohol, however, the feeling doesn't last and is replaced by a new craving. Eventually this need for power can become so strong, it will lead to heightened forms of abuse, including rape.

DATE RAPE

Gloria considered Morris a hunk. A successful athlete, he was one of the most popular guys in school. So when he asked her to a party at his older brother's fraternity house, she immediately said yes. Morris suggested they meet for coffee at his place an hour before going to the party. While they were waiting for Morris's brother to arrive, Morris kept putting brandy in her coffee. Before long, Gloria felt silly and laughed at everything he said. Then he started talking about sex. Out of the blue, he asked her about the shape of her breasts. She was embarrassed, but didn't want to seem like a child so she tried to change the subject.

Morris finally admitted that his brother wasn't going to show up. He offered to take her to a movie, but he didn't have enough cash. Within moments, Morris was fixing her another drink and telling Gloria how attractive he found her.

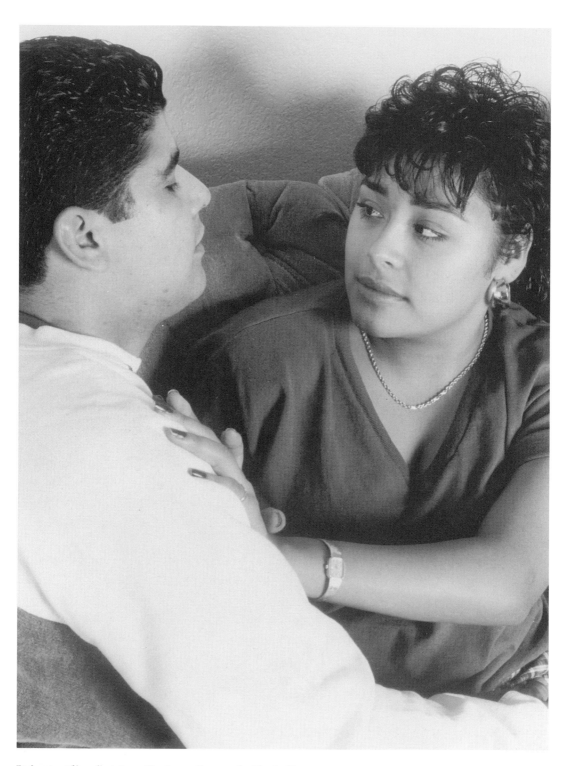

It is startling but true that nearly one-half of all rapes are commited by someone the victim knows. Many times the rape occurs on a date, when the rapist maintains that the woman wanted to have sex.

He kissed her, and Gloria kissed him back. Then he started telling her what a good lover he was. Gloria became nervous, and said she wanted to go home. Morris exploded. He said that if she didn't have sex with him, he'd tell everyone they did it anyway. Gloria called him a pig and started for the door. Morris grabbed her, hit her, then held her on the floor and raped her.

When he was done, he gave her $20 and told her to take a cab home. She threw it in his face and ran outside. Crying and stunned, she managed to walk home.

The next day, Gloria called a rape counseling hotline. The woman Gloria spoke to asked her to tell about the incident and made suggestions about what she should do. She recommended that Gloria talk to the police, but Gloria was afraid.

Over the next few weeks, Gloria continued to call the hotline. She spoke with several different women volunteers, most of whom had been rape victims. Some said they had reported their rapes to the police. Some had testified in court against the men who raped them. A few had not told anyone except hotline callers of having been raped.

One evening Gloria decided to tell her parents what happened. To her surprise, her mother believed her right away. Her father took it hard. He was very angry with Morris and wanted to know where he lived. Eventually, he calmed down.

Gloria finally took a pregnancy test and tests for a sexual disease. When the results came back negative, she cried with relief. Then she and her parents met with an attorney who specialized in cases involving rape and sexual abuse. The attorney explained that if she prosecuted Morris for rape, Gloria would have to testify in front of several strangers and tell everything that happened. Morris's attorney would try to discredit Gloria's story and convince the jury that Gloria agreed to have sex. Her attorney recommended that Gloria talk to a therapist first before making a decision.

After receiving counseling, Gloria made up a list of reasons for not prosecuting Morris, and reasons for doing so. Despite the obstacles, Gloria decided to bring charges against him.

"I can't know how things will go," she said, "but I think that it will help me to deal with what has happened if I use the system to fight back against him in this way. Thanks to all the people I've talked to, I've been able to stop blaming myself almost entirely for what happened. I've decided to do it for me, but it also seems like I can do it for others, too. If another woman learns of this situation and decides to bring charges against her rapist, or if a guy learns about the case and is scared into cleaning up his act, it will be worth it. Maybe I will be protecting some other women from Morris's charms."

When Morris' case was finally heard in criminal court, it took a jury less than two days of deliberations to convict him of rape. Morris received a five-year sentence and was ordered to pay for Gloria's psychological counseling.

RAPE BY A STRANGER

Ruthie, a 17-year-old high school student, attended an evening event. Knowing it wouldn't be over until after ten, Ruthie's father made sure she had money for a phone call. Since her father had been in bed most of the week with the flu, Ruthie decided to let him rest. She decided to walk home instead. As she passed a park, a man jumped out from behind some bushes and tackled her.

"At first I thought something had fallen on me," she said. "Then, when I felt his hand, I thought, my God, it's a man. I didn't really think about being raped. I just thought this guy tackled me for no reason and I got mad. I was in the middle of slugging and kicking him when he said something that made me realize that he was going to rape me. If I hadn't already been so angry, I might have gotten really scared. He started saying things about how he didn't want to hurt me. I scratched at his face because I was trying to poke him in the eye. I thought that if he couldn't see me I might get away. That made him mad so he started swearing at me. I swore back. Words were coming out of my mouth that I didn't even know I knew."

To her relief and surprise, Ruthie's attacker let go and ran to a van across the street. She was not seriously hurt, but was shook up. After calling her dad, they went to the police station and Ruthie filed a report and described her attacker.

WHO IS SAFE?

About 45 percent of all rapes are committed by someone known, however slightly, to the victim (other authorities say it may be as high as 60 percent). Nearly 33 percent of all rapes occur in the victim's home. Therefore, a woman who doesn't go out by herself late at night and avoids strange men can still be in danger of rape.

Although about 100,000 rapes are reported in America each year, they are only a small percentage of the actual number of rapes that occur. To make matters more horrifying, the number of rapes that actually occur are far fewer than those attempted. There is no way to know exactly how many rapes are committed, attempted, or accomplished and unreported.

TEENAGE RAPISTS

Juveniles are very often both the victims and the perpetrators of rape. While rapists come from all age groups and economic backgrounds, studies show that most rapists are males between the ages of 15 and 24. It is no surprise, then, that females in that age group are frequently sexually assaulted and raped. The young males who commit these crimes do not understand that "no" means "no." Our society presents the idea that anything goes, that nothing is forbidden. Many kids have never been told that certain types of behavior cannot be tolerated.

Why do so many young men commit rape? Males typically become sexually mature at about age 13 or 14. However, many teenage males have never been taught to consider the feelings of others and are unprepared for sexual responsibility. Growing up in a society where aggressive and sometimes violent behavior is rewarded, where they are subjected to many persistent male myths about females, and where they are exposed to popular cultural images that depict females as objects of desire instead of as individuals, males are easily confused and persuaded that it is what they want that counts. Lacking information, role models, and experience, males often become sexually active without having a clear understanding of the difference between consensual sex and rape.

WHY DO RAPES GO UNREPORTED?

Why don't more women report rape? Experts say women most often offer five reasons for their reluctance:

Shame. Most women tend to blame themselves in some way for what happened. The loss of control over their own bodies experienced by rape victims seems to produce a powerful sense of shame. One counselor puts it this way. "We are deeply conditioned to believe that our survival depends on our ability to control what happens to our bodies. When rape happens it seems to prove that we cannot exercise that control, and we often feel this powerful shame. It is as if, somehow, we have failed to safeguard our very lives."

A desire to protect the rapist. Some rape counselors say that while many people who are raped hate the rapist and hope that he will die in jail or suffer some horrible punishment, other date rape victims—particularly those who tend to blame themselves—often find it hard to hate the rapist, especially if they knew or dated him.

Fear of not being believed. Many rape victims worry about what the accused rapist will do when confronted by the authorities. It is often the victim's word against the rapist. Will a jury think that the victim is just being spiteful? Will they think the victim asked for it?

Blaming the victim. Experts say that in rape-related cases, many people are ready to believe that women who are raped used bad judgment. Some people think that people who are raped are fools for having dated someone capable of rape. Some people think that acquaintance rape or date rape only occurs when the female goes back on her agreement to have sex, or the female gets mad at the rapist afterward.

The lengthy legal process. Criminal trials are often lengthy and unnerving, especially to the victim who must testify under stressful conditions.

Despite these concerns, victims of sexual crimes should still report them, to prevent others from becoming victims.

Why are so many females between age 15 and 25 raped? Like males, many young females lack a clear understanding of sexuality. Having little sexual experience, they are often unprepared for the ferocity and persistence of the male sex drive. They are anxious to please members of the opposite sex and often share a willingness to take risks that older women with more experience might not take.

Each gender has different ideas about the nature of sex. Males are conditioned to think of sex in terms of their own pleasure. Believing that females are objects for that pleasure, many males seek sexual release through rape. This can be date rape, rape of a stranger, or even rape of a family member.

SEXUAL ABUSE

Eleven-year-old Crystal loved her dad, but she felt funny about the way he hugged and touched her. His affection didn't feel the same as the hugs and kisses that came from her mother or her grandparents. She tried a couple of times to tell her mother that there was something wrong with the way her dad touched her, but her mother told her it was just her imagination.

Many parents have a hard time believing that their son or daughter could be suffering sexual abuse at the hands of a spouse.

When Crystal's mother had to go into the hospital for three days, her dad said he wanted her to sleep in his bed to help keep him warm. Crystal didn't want to and pretended to be sick. Later she heard her dad come into her room. He asked how she was feeling, and then got into bed with her.

At first Crystal pretended to sleep. Her dad put his arms around her. After a while, he started moving his hands to places on her body where she knew they shouldn't be. She was frozen with fear.

The next day Crystal felt ashamed and scared, but didn't know who she could talk to. For two more nights her dad came to her room. When Crystal's mother came home she was still quite sick, so Crystal decided not to say anything about what had happened. When her mother felt better, Crystal tried to tell her about her father's actions. Her mother didn't believe her and asked Crystal what kind of television programs she had been watching the last week.

Crystal felt rejected and confused. She started spending a lot of time in her room alone. One Saturday morning a few weeks later, Crystal's mother had to go out for a few hours. Crystal was told to stay home and clean the garage. After a time, her father suggested that they take a break together by sitting in the car and listening to the radio. She said she had to finish her chores. Her father became angry. He forced her into the car and had sex with her. Her father said that if she ever told anyone, he would get in the car and go away and that she and her mother would be forced to live on welfare in a bad neighborhood.

Crystal became depressed and withdrawn. She hardly spoke to her parents. She imagined what it would be like to die. One morning she took a bottle of her mother's tranquilizers to school and swallowed them all with orange juice. During her first class she had to go to the bathroom, where she threw up and then collapsed. A teacher found her and called the paramedics.

Crystal was lucky; she could have died. Since attempted suicide is a clear signal that someone is having a serious problem, people began asking Crystal to talk about what was bothering her. Eventually, her mother believed her, and soon she filed for a divorce from Crystal's father and started undergoing therapy. Crystal's father is facing criminal charges for raping his daughter.

There is perhaps no more lonely feeling in the world than trying to live with the shame and humiliation of being molested by a trusted family member—especially when it is a father or mother. Certainly it might have made her feel less isolated, but it would not have made Crystal feel any better to know that many other young people have been and continue to be molested by parents, siblings, relatives, and family friends. By the end of the 1980s, nearly 750,000 American women acknowledged that their fathers or brothers had sexually molested them when they were young. Even more chilling, sexual abuse in the family is often accompanied by other forms of physical violence.

Experts say that many fathers who sexually abuse their children are physically abusive toward their wives. By regularly abusing the mother, a father is able to keep her too frightened to go to authorities for help. Very often the mother is incapable of doing anything about sexual abuse committed by the father. Any action taken against an abusive father won't begin until the young victims go outside the family for help.

TALKING TO SOMEONE

If you are being sexually molested or abused at home or somewhere else, whether by a parent, relative, or family friend, you need to understand you can change your circumstances for the better.

Just as the situations faced by others in this chapter were horrifying and unique to them, so your own situation is unique to you. What the people in this chapter have in common is that despite the horrible things that happened to them, each spoke out in order to escape from an intolerable situation. In doing so, they were able to begin the road to recovery.

If a family conference is unheard of in your house—if you cannot trust someone because they have sexually abused you or a sibling—then find another adult you can talk to.

If you have been raped, molested, or abused in any way, the best thing you can do for yourself is to determine which adult you know who will listen to and understand your story. That person may not be your mother, your sister, your aunt, or anyone who is a part of your immediate family. Who else can you talk to? Who can you really trust? How do you feel about your teacher? If not this year's teacher, how about last year's? Do you have a guidance counselor or a gym teacher you like and trust? Does your school principal seem like a strong and solid person who might help you seek protection from abuse? How about a family priest, minister, or rabbi?

If you can't think of anyone you can talk to right away, look in the phone book and find an abuse hotline or a crisis center's phone number and call it. Libraries also contain information and advice based on the experiences of others. A good librarian can show you how to get in touch with organizations dedicated to helping people in trouble.

Do not be afraid to ask. You have a right to be helped, comforted, taken care of, and to feel better.

7

FINDING ALTERNATIVES
AND SOLUTIONS

*There're plenty of things adults and kids can do to
stop violence.*
—Kyle, age 17

W e have seen that some juveniles experience
anger problems and are drawn to violence as a
way of expressing their anger. Some juveniles, however,
are drawn to violence as a form of excitement—a way
of adding a sense of creative excitement or self-
expression to their lives. What about those who are
bored and underchallenged by their lives?

In 1981, at the age of 26, an artist named Tim
Rollins began teaching at I.S. 52 in the South Bronx to
support his art career. For the most part his students
were of Hispanic background. Many were dyslexic
and had difficulty reading. Most were unfamiliar
with any art other than the graffiti in their own
neighborhood. Rollins soon saw that more than a
few of his most talented students were living in
poverty and dabbling in drugs. Some were also
bored and unrecognized at home. Rollins responded
by forming an artistically talented group known as
the Kids of Survival (KOS) and the Art and
Knowledge Workshop.

In the beginning Rollins had to scrounge for
paper and pencils, simple materials that would help
students interested in doing something creative on

*Many gang members in Los Angeles have tried to make peace in
the city since the riots of 1992. These gang members meet in parks
to try and find solutions to the problem of juvenile violence.*

their lunch hour. Then he applied for and received a grant from the National Endowment for the Arts. With the grant money he was able to rent a studio, acquire more supplies, and begin working with students on group projects. Soon the KOS was selling paintings, sculptures, and mixed media artworks.

KOS projects are collaborative. Rather than influencing his artistic young friends to create art that he likes, Rollins introduces students to books and ideas that excite their imagination, then guides them in formulating ways to turn their ideas into art. Their creations have been exhibited and sold by some of the top galleries in the world.

Recently Rollins has been negotiating with the city of New York to form his own art school, a 25,000-square-foot facility that Rollins hopes will serve as "a beacon of hope to the community." He wants the school to accommodate at least 40 students, offer a variety of night classes to neighborhood residents, and bring in famous and successful artists as guest teachers and lecturers.

Well-known art collectors are paying up to $150,000 for an original collaborative painting or work of art by Rollins and his young artists. The prestigious Museum of Modern Art in New York City has acquired KOS works for its permanent collection.

Many of the young KOS artists who had never before been out of New York are now traveling around the world, telling people in other countries about their work and meeting influential people in the international art world. This program could be a role model for other disadvantaged young people around the country who exhibit their creative talents in more unorthodox ways.

EXPANDING HORIZONS

Outward Bound, an organization formed in Great Britain in 1941 by an educator named Kurt Hahn, is dedicated to introducing young people to the rigors of outdoor life. Every year more than 30,000 people from all over the world attend camps in remote areas of Colorado, Maine, North Carolina, Minnesota, and Oregon, where they are challenged physically in ways they never dreamed of. The Outward Bound strategy involves teaching self-reliance and teamwork to small groups of individuals by presenting them with wilderness survival problems most people rarely—if ever—face in city life. In learning to climb rocks and mountains, navigate whitewater rapids, build shelters, and survive in the wilderness with scant food and tools, students gain self-confidence and an ability to tap into inner resources they never knew they had.

Carmen, a 17-year-old who lives in New York City, had this to say about her experiences in the Adirondack Mountains. "Intense hiking, canoeing, rock climbing—I never did that kind of stuff. It gave me a chance to see life in a different way, not just on the streets."

Over 1,700 thoroughly trained instructors lead groups of eight to 12 participants through action-oriented activities that last from three days to three weeks. Urban programs that focus on skills valuable in city settings are also offered. These urban programs mostly revolve around service such as environmental cleanup or working with senior citizens.

Outward Bound is a nonprofit organization, and it raises scholarship money and allocates it to individual schools. Every year nearly $1.5 million in scholarship money goes to about 25 percent of the participants. Since it costs an average of $24,000 to imprison one person for one year, it makes sense for city, county, and state governments to enact programs for at-risk youths as a way of rewarding those who stay out of trouble. This is also one method of providing career opportunities for people who want to help combat juvenile violence.

Organizations such as Outward Bound help young people develop self-esteem by teaching them survival skills and self-reliance in the wilderness.

Not everyone is creative or wants to be an artist. Not everyone benefits equally by roughing it in the wilderness. Some at-risk juveniles are not especially angry or underchallenged. Many young people simply long for a sense of being important. Living in communities where they really don't relate to anyone other than themselves, young people often turn to one another and try to please their friends. But what if there were organizations that really valued their talents and offered them friendship and opportunity? In fact, there are.

NEW FRIENDSHIPS

More than a dozen years ago a woman named Kathy Levin took a look around and saw a large population of middle school students, many of whom were from single-parent families and surrounded by the temptations of drugs and violence. Levin also saw something else—a large population of senior citizens confined to nursing homes. Although the two groups were many years apart, Levin saw that they had a great deal in common: Most notably, a lot of time on their hands and a feeling of being unwanted. This proved to be the inspiration behind the Baltimore-based program known as Magic-Me.

Today, Magic-Me has spread to some 30 cities in the United States and even has programs in London and Paris. Magic-Me is a three-year voluntary program geared to middle school students who, while participating in an ordinary middle school curriculum, also visit selected nursing homes on a regular basis. New students and nursing home residents often "break the ice" by playing volleyball games with balloons. Eventually the students pair up with individual seniors and are left free to develop friendships.

After visiting the homes, students participate in "reflection periods," where they are encouraged to think about their experiences. They are asked to keep a journal about their visits and write down their thoughts about their senior friends. These journals, which often deal with vital life problems touching on love, jealousy, possessiveness, sickness, and death, are read by group leaders and often become topics for discussion. Although the program only runs through the eighth grade, many graduating students continue their friendships with their special seniors for years after their participation in the program has come to an end.

Most young people benefit from the special feeling of being needed by others. Juveniles who lack family role models, however, usually want the friendship of someone older and more experienced—someone they can look up to. One of the oldest and most successful groups that tries to remedy this situation is an organization known as the Big Brothers and Big Sisters of America.

Big Brothers and Big Sisters of America brings together young people who need a mother or father figure with adults who want to share time and experiences with them.

In Big Brother/Big Sister programs, boys and girls between ages 7 and 18 are matched with older males and females who share their interests. If you want to become involved in such a program, have one of your parents or your legal guardian make an appointment with the Big Brother or Big Sister office nearest you (see listing in back of book). You will be asked about your background and special interests so that the organization can match you with a Big Brother or Big Sister who shares some of your interests.

Adults become Big Brothers or Big Sisters through a similar interview process. They are screened for interests and background, making it unlikely that you'll be teamed up with someone who will be harmful to you. The group does not advertise, and Big Brothers and Big Sisters are not paid for their services. For that reason, adults who volunteer are usually motivated by their own goals and desire to help and share with young people.

The group requires that Big Brothers or Sisters devote a minimum amount of time to activities with their assigned "little" brothers or sisters. This time consists of shared activities and regular telephone calls. Little brothers and sisters are also often taken to visit the work places of their big brothers and sisters, enabling them to see and understand something of the "world of work." Also, big brothers and sisters remember birthdays and holidays.

How long a young person has to wait to be given a big brother or big sister varies from community to community. Although efforts are made to team up a youngster with a partner right away, sometimes there is as much as a three-month wait. However, during this waiting period, young people who have been interviewed and are ready to participate are immediately drawn into the "big brother family" by becoming involved in group activities held at various Big Brother and Big Sister headquarters.

More than 500 communities in the United States have Big Brother or Big Sister programs dedicated to providing young people with stable adult friendships. Some of these groups offer special programs aimed at helping youngsters with learning disabilities, or those who have already been in some kind of trouble with the law. All of them provide an opportunity for a young boy or girl to make a new friend who will help him or her grow and experience new things.

FAMILY MATTERS

If experts are right and juvenile violence begins at home, then home is surely the place to begin resolving the problem. In the belief that the key to a better, less violent future society is in the hands of society's present and future parents, some groups have begun to teach vital parenting skills.

Education for Parenting was started in 1979 by Sally Scattergood, a teacher at the Germantown Friends School in Philadelphia, Pennsylvania. Her goal was to develop a curriculum to teach children what it means to be a responsible, caring parent. She was influenced by the work of Henri Parens, a psychiatrist who was convinced that very young children could be taught a lot about child-rearing and then pass along the benefits of what they learned to their own peers and children. Today, nine Philadelphia schools, all located in poor ghetto areas, have adopted or adapted Scattergood's program.

Along with a traditional curriculum, middle school students are regularly exposed to babies and very young children and encouraged to interact with them. New mothers and pregnant mothers are brought into the classroom for discussions about the importance of nutrition for pregnant mothers, and the potentially harmful effects of alcohol and drugs on unborn children. Small children just beginning to speak are brought into class and students are given a chance to discuss important topics like praise, self-esteem, and discipline problems. The effects of spanking are discussed, and students are encouraged to establish positive methods of communicating with the visiting toddlers.

Fourth and fifth grade students at the Germantown School spend time observing babies and parents who attend a parent-infant support group. Eventually, each child is assigned a baby to observe and reports his or her observations on a worksheet. By the sixth grade, many students are judged ready for caretaker responsibilities.

Once a week for about 12 weeks, students are paired with individual toddlers at the day-care center run by the school for its employees. The students also meet with the toddlers' parents, make toys for "their" children, and write reports on their successes, which they then present to the parents of the tots. Many of the participants are 12- and 13-year-old juveniles of African-American descent who have grown up without fathers. Since some seventh and eighth grade girls are already getting pregnant, other Philadelphia schools are taking a look at the many potential benefits of this program.

A NATIONAL PROBLEM

Deborah Prothrow-Stith is a medical doctor who believes that a medical profession willing to consider smoking a national health problem should also treat juvenile violence as a national health problem. With that in mind, she co-founded the Violence Prevention Project at Boston City Hospital in Massachusetts, and later helped develop the Curriculum to Prevent Adolescent Violence, which now has programs in many of the nation's largest cities. Prothrow-Stith believes that just as smokers invite health problems by lighting up, juveniles often behave in ways that put them at risk of becoming involved in violence.

In the Curriculum to Prevent Adolescent Violence, young people are trained in anger control and taught how to replace violence with assertive behavior and negotiation. Participants act out skits intended to teach them the

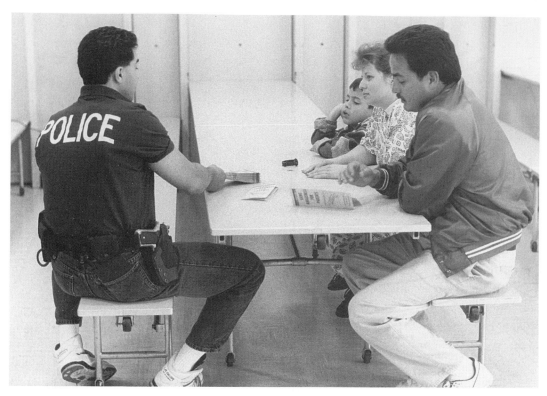

Parents and police are becoming more involved in programs that help stop juvenile violence before it starts, including special meetings held in schools, churches, and community centers.

value of clear talk and dignified compromise. Film, videos, books, and other media are used to deglamorize violence. Just as juvenile violence has many causes, Dr. Prothrow-Stith believes it also has many solutions. What's required, she says, is an all-out effort by government, churches, schools, the media, community organizations, and industry to inform and encourage young people to control violent behavior.

However, programs organized by adults are not enough to stem the tide of juvenile violence. While Dr. Prothrow-Stith seeks to reach out to adults and institutions on a broad policy-making front, she also works one-on-one with juveniles, encouraging them to do what they can for themselves and applauding the direct individual efforts made by large numbers of people.

Many broken families begin when young women have babies and are then abandoned by the young fathers who discover they are ill-prepared for fatherhood. Some hospitals and schools have begun programs in an effort to reach young fathers, convincing them that an interest in child development is not against the macho code. Teacher Lou Howort began teaching Child Development and Parenting to eleventh and twelfth graders at the High School for the Humanities, and versions of his class are now being taught at 33 high schools in New York City.

TIME TO ACT

If there is a violence problem in your life, if you are afraid at school and on the streets, if your parents have abused you or have been violent in disciplining you, you can take action to help yourself. If you are abusing your own children, you can learn how to be a good parent by managing your anger and frustration and applying praise and persuasion rather than blame and physical punishment. If you plan to have children one day, you can learn now how to stop using violence or the threat of violence to get your own way—at home or with friends and on the streets.

Together we can make our cities and towns less violent places in which babies, teens, and adults of all races and age groups can live in peace. But we have to start with the most difficult part of that task. We have to start with ourselves.

FINDING HELP

In the back of this book you will find a list of hotlines and special organizations that specialize in dealing with juvenile and family violence and various forms of abuse. Phone numbers that begin with 800 are free calls and, while your call may be answered by someone in another city, the telephone you are using will not be charged for a long distance call.

If you do not find the organization you expected to find in your own community, don't despair. Many, if not most, of these organizations have special contacts in other cities and communities. Also check out the "Social Service Organizations" heading in your telephone book's yellow pages. Chances are good that you will soon be talking with someone eager to help you.

ADDITIONAL RESOURCES

Phone numbers to call: 800 numbers are toll-free calls. There is no charge for calling a telephone number that begins with 800.

Action/Pride, The National Resource Center (800) 241-7946.

Child Help USA (800) 4-A-CHILD.

Cocaine Helpline (800) COCAINE.

Family Service America, Inc. (800) 221-2681.

Narcotics Education, Washington, D.C. (800) 548-8700.

National Association of Homes for Children (800) 843-6242.

National Domestic Violence Hotline (800) 333-7233 (affiliated with 1,200 domestic violence shelters nationwide).

National Federation of Parents for Drug Free Youth (800) 554-KIDS.

New York City Division of Substance Abuse Services (800) 522-5353.

New York State Council on Alcoholism (800) ALC-ALLS.

Parents Anonymous (800) 421-0353.

Organizations to write to:

American Association for Marriage and Family Therapy, 1717 K Street NW, Washington, D.C. 20006 (202) 429-1825 (Publishes a *Consumer's Guide to Family Therapy* free; send them a self-addressed stamped envelope).

American Youth Work Center, 1751 N Street NW, Washington, D.C. 20036 (Provides state-by-state listings of shelters in the North American Directory of Programs for Runaways).

Big Brothers/Big Sisters of America, 230 N. 13th St., Philadelphia, PA 19107-1551, (215) 567-7000 (Check local listings, too).

Boys and Girls Clubs of America, 771 First Avenue, New York, NY 10017 (212)351-5900 (This organization has 1,200 local facilities nationwide).

Child Abuse Listening Mediation, P.O. Box 718, Santa Barbara, CA 93102 (805)682-1366.

Child Welfare League of America, 440 First Street NW, Washington, DC 20001 (202) 638-2952 (Provides lists of approved shelters in A Directory of Member Agencies, available at libraries).

Clearing House on Child Abuse and Neglect Information, P.O. Box 1182, Washington, D.C. 20013 (703) 821-2086.

Institute for Mental Health Initiatives Channeling Children's Anger, 4545 42nd St. NW, Washington, DC 20016 (202) 364-7111.

Magic-Me, 808 N. Charles St., Baltimore, MD 21201 (410) 837-0900.

Male Youth Enhancement Project, 1510 9th St. NW, Washington, DC 20001 (202}332-0213.

Outward Bound USA, 384 Field Point Road, Greenwich, CT 06830-7098 (800) 243-8520.

National Center for the Prosecution of Child Abuse, 1033 N. Fairfax St., Suite 200, Alexandra, VA 22314 (703) 739-0321.

National Committee for the Prevention of Child Abuse, 3325 S. Michigan Ave., Suite 950, Chicago, IL 60604 (312) 663-3520.

National Crime Prevention Council, 1700 K Street NW, Second Floor, Washington, DC 20006 (202) 466-6272.

New York City Department of Juvenile Justice, 365 Broadway, New York, NY 10013 (212) 925-7779.

Resolving Conflict Creatively, 163 Third Avenue, Suite 239, New York, NY 10003 (212) 260-6290.

Toughlove, P.O. Box 1069, Doylestown, PA 18901 (215) 348-7090.

FOR FURTHER READING

Arnstein, Jeffrey. *We Grow Up Fast Nowadays: Conversations with a New Generation.* Los Angeles, CA: Lowell House, 1991.

Blake, James L. *Common Sense in a Complex World.* Evanston, WY: Common Sense Information Publishing, 1989.

Bode, Janet. *The Voices of Rape.* New York, NY: Franklin Watts, 1990.

Booher, Dianna Daniels. *Making Friends with Yourself and Others.* New York, NY: Julian Messner, 1982.

Brown, Gene. *Violence on America's Streets.* Brookfield, CT: The Millbrook Press, 1992.

Cooney, Judith. *Coping with Sexual Abuse.* New York, NY: The Rosen Publishing Group, 1987.

Davis, James R. *Help Me, I'm Hurt: the Child Abuse Handbook.* Dubuque, IA: Kendall/Hunt Publishing, 1982.

Kyte, Kathy S. *Play It Safe: The Kids' Guide to Personal Safety and Crime Prevention.* New York, NY: Alfred A. Knopf, 1983.

Laiken, Deidre S. and Alan J. Schneider. *Listen to Me, I'm Angry.* New York, NY: Lothrop, Lee & Shepard, 1980.

Langone, John. *Violence: Our Fastest Growing Public Health Problem.* Boston, MA: Little, Brown and Company, 1984.

Mantice, Jim. *Fifty Simple Ways to Protect Yourself from Burglars, Thieves, Muggers, Con-Artists.* Evanston, IL: Walnut Grove Publishers, 1992.

McFarland, Rhoda. *Coping Through Assertiveness.* New York, NY: The Rosen Publishing Group, 1986.

Miedzian, Myriam. *Boys Will Be Boys: Breaking the Link between Masculinity and Violence.* New York, NY: Doubleday, 1991.

Smith, Sandra Lee. *Discovering Your Own Space.* New York, NY: The Rosen Publishing Group, 1992.

Thomas, Piri. *Down These Mean Streets.* New York, NY: Vintage Books, 1991.

Wesson, McClenahan Carolyn. *Teen Troubles: How to Keep Them from Becoming Tragedies.* New York, NY: Walker Publishing Company, Inc., 1988.

Wormser, Richard. *Lifers: Learn the Truth at the Expense of Our Sorrow.* New York, NY: Julian Messner, 1991.

GLOSSARY

Abuse. Harmful behavior of one or more people toward another. Abuse can take many forms: sexual abuse, most often when young females are sexually touched, molested, or raped by bigger, older males; physical abuse, when someone is beaten or otherwise injured by another; verbal abuse is or can be violent in its effect on another's self-esteem or sense of well-being.

Aggression. Behavior characterized by direct action in pursuit of a particular goal. Aggressiveness is valued because it encourages behavior that can lead to prompt results. Socially unacceptable aggressiveness is behavior that ignores the safety, rights, and well-being of others and can lead to violence.

"Blaming the victim." A common social tendency to criticize the victim for causing a crime. Blaming the victim is often the expression of an individual's or society's frustration and insensitivity. It results in little or no action being taken against the person who created the harm in the first place.

Conditioning. The not-so-obvious factors that may cause a particular behavior. Rewarding behavior is a form of conditioning since it encourages repetition in expec-

tation of further rewards. Repeated verbal abuse is a form of negative conditioning.

Date rape. Rape that occurs on a date, most often when the girl feels she knows the boy well enough to trust him. Date rape is a common and difficult problem, since in many cases the victim is reluctant to charge her "friend" with the crime. Because the line between violence and lack of consent can be hazy, date rape victims often wrongly blame themselves. Hence, many date rapes go unreported.

Empathy. The capacity to identify with another or feel his or her feelings. People with empathy are not likely to hit others in the head with a baseball bat because they can "empathize" with how it would feel to be hit. People lacking in empathy may give in to their frustrations and hit someone because they are unable to relate the experience back to themselves.

Juvenile. Characteristic of youth or young people. By law, a juvenile is a person under the age of 18. An adult is anyone over age 18.

Mediation. The process of settling disputes or conflicts through discussion, compromise, and agreement with the assistance of a neutral third party, known as the mediator. Mediators listen to all aspects of the dispute, reduce it to essentials, promote tolerant views of differences, and help find a solution agreeable to all. The basic rule of mediation is that each party can win something, provided he or she is willing to give up something.

Rape. Definitions and rape laws vary from state to state, but there is broad agreement that rape is vaginal, anal, or oral sex forced on an individual or individuals by one or more individuals. See also Abuse and Date Rape.

Role model. A real or imagined figure whose behavior is presented or perceived as desirable and who will inspire imitation. Role models can be anyone—a mother or father, brother or sister, or a professional athlete or rock star.

Self-esteem. The way a person feels about herself or himself. Individuals with high self-esteem have confidence and believe in their worth and abilities. Individuals with low self-esteem have feelings of unworthiness and believe they will fail.

Testosterone. The hormone that determines the gender of a human embryo. Males have high levels of testosterone. Females have lower levels. Individuals with high testosterone levels tend to be athletic, favor physical activity, and show tendencies to be more aggressive and violent than individuals with lower levels.

Violence. Physical force or strength, often characterized by suddeness or intensity. As used here, the unjust, callous, or careless use of strength or power that violates another person's rights, physical body, and/or his sense of well-being. A threat can be violent because it violates a person's right to feel safe. Use of strength or power that violates another.

INDEX

A

abuse
    of children, 9, 11, 14
    in the family, 11-12
    and persecuting groups, 64-65
    sexual, 76-78
    of spouses, 9, 11, 17
    statistics on, 14
abusers, 70
abusive relationships, 67-69, 70
alcohol
    and family abuse, 11-12, 14
    and self-esteem, 12
    and underage drinking, 53-55
arrests
    for challenging authority, 53-55
    juvenile, 5, 37
    of males, 24
    for weapons violations, 37
Art and Knowledge Workshop, 81

B

bias, 64-65
Big Brothers/Big Sisters of America, 25-26, 84-86
Bloods, 44, 46
bullies, 31-33

C

Center to Prevent Handgun Violence, 38
children
    and physical discipline, 9
    who attack parents, 9, 14
Crips, 44, 46
Curriculum to Prevent Adolescent Violence, 87-88

D

date rape, 71-73
drive-by shootings, 43-44
drugs
    and family abuse, 11-12, 14
    and self-esteem, 12
    possession of, 53-55

E

Education for Parenting, 86-87
"emotional literacy," 38-39

F

families
    and abuse, 14-16
    single-parent, 26
    and sexual abuse, 76-78
    and tough love, 60-61
    without fathers, 26

G

gang(s)
    avoiding, 47
    clothing, 47
    and drug dealing, 46
    life, 45-47
    recruiting new members, 46-47
    -related murders, 45
    and self-esteem, 13
    and turf, 46
    in U.S. cities, 45
guns
    arrests related to, 37-38
    and counseling, 38
    and gang-related murders, 45
    in school, 33, 37-38
    used in crimes, 51

J

juvenile(s)
    in abusive relationships, 67-69
    attracted to gangs, 46-47
    challenging authority, 53
    death by gunshot, 37-38
    defined, 22
    how to avoid
        misunderstandings, 53-55
        violence, 50-51
    and interracial relationships, 58-60
    role models, 26
    and senior citizens, 84
    using art to express anger, 81

3 9510 2002 3908 8

364.36
B23

Barden, Renardo.
    Juvenile violence

14.95

PLAINFIELD PUBLIC LIBRARY
8th ST. AT PARK AVE.
PLAINFIELD, NJ 07060

GAYLORD RG

WITHDRAWN